RETAIL DESIGN INTER-NATIONAL

FOCUS: RE-USE

JONS MESSEDAT

avedition

CONTENTS

INTRODUCTION: RE-USE IN RETAIL　4
Dr. Jons Messedat

VACANCY MEANS STANDSTILL –
CITY STRUCTURE: HOW DO WE NOW SUSTAINABLY
REBUILD OUR CITY CENTRES?　8
Albert Achammer, ATP architekten ingenieure

A NETWORKED APPROACH TO BUILDING
FOR THE FUTURE　14
Jutta Blocher, blocher partners

CULTIVATING THE FUTURE OF RETAIL
WITH EDUCATION AND INNOVATION　20
Gabi Stumvoll & Dr. Maximilian Perez, Rid Stiftung

SPACES

BYD PIONEER STORE, GERMANY　26
ATELIER BRÜCKNER, Stuttgart

MAISON M-I-D 1985, JAPAN　30
CURIOSITY, Tokyo

GROHE WATER EXPERIENCE CENTER, GERMANY　34
D'art Design Gruppe, Neuss / LIXIL Global Design

ROTTLER EXKLUSIV, GERMANY　38
HEIKAUS Architektur GmbH, Stuttgart

SALON VERDE, AUSTRIA　42
umdasch The Store Makers, Amstetten

MEST MARZIPAN LÜBECK, GERMANY　46
D.S.D.5 Planungsgesellschaft mbH, Mülheim a.d. Ruhr

BUCHERER FINE JEWELLERY, GERMANY　50
blocher partners, Stuttgart

SENSAI FLAGSHIP STORE SHANGHAI, CHINA　54
CURIOSITY, Tokyo

CONCEPT STORE BY STAUDE, GERMANY　58
NOMAH interior solutions, Hanover

SCHÖFFEL SHOWROOM, GERMANY　64
Konrad Knoblauch GmbH, Markdorf

ELBE RAEDEREI, GERMANY　68
Theodor Schemberg Einrichtungen GmbH, Mettingen

MARKTKAUF CENTER WISMAR, GERMANY　72
Kinzel Architecture, Schermbeck

SC FREIBURG, GERMANY　76
CBA Clemens Bachmann Architekten, Munich

ONVIO, GERMANY　80
Theodor Schemberg Einrichtungen GmbH, Mettingen

DIE MUSTANG GRUPPE BRAND BOX　84
Konrad Knoblauch GmbH, Markdorf

ANNEMARIE BÖRLIND
COSMETIC DISPLAY FAMILY, GERMANY　88
ARNO GmbH, Wolfschlugen

EDEKA HAFENMARKT STROETMANN, GERMANY　92
Interstore AG, Zurich

BETTENRID, GERMANY　96
umdasch The Store Makers, Amstetten

JEWELLERY PLETZSCH, GERMANY　100
HEIKAUS Architektur GmbH, Stuttgart

POGGENPOHL SHANGHAI
EXPERIENCE CENTER, CHINA　104
Ippolito Fleitz Group – Identity Architects, Stuttgart

MELT SEASON FLAGSHIP
AT TAIYUAN ROAD, CHINA　108
Mlkk Studio Limited, Hong Kong

NIO HOUSE DUSSELDORF, GERMANY　112
Vizona GmbH, Weil am Rhein

SV DARMSTADT 98, GERMANY　116
CBA Clemens Bachmann Architekten, Munich

QUADFLIEG, GERMANY　120
Theodor Schemberg Einrichtungen GmbH, Mettingen

CONTENTS

GENESIS STUDIOS, SWITZERLAND / GERMANY   124
Mint Architecture, Zurich, Part of the ATP Group

PUPPENKÖNIG, GERMANY   128
umdasch The Store Makers, Amstetten

BUILDINGS

DALIAN HUANAN MIXC ONE MALL, CHINA   134
Ippolito Fleitz Group – Identity Architects, Stuttgart

HAGEMEYER, GERMANY   140
blocher partners, Stuttgart

EDEKA ADEBAHR, GERMANY   144
Ansorg GmbH, Mülheim a. d. Ruhr

KRÖPELINER STRASSE 64, GERMANY   148
ATP architekten ingenieure, Nuremberg

PALLADIUM MALL AHMEDABAD, INDIA   152
blocher partners, Stuttgart / Ahmedabad

RÄBGASS SHOPPING CENTER, SWITZERLAND   156
Mint Architecture, Zurich, Part of the ATP Group

WOLLHAUS HEILBRONN, GERMANY   160
blocher partners, Stuttgart

THE AUTHORS   164

EXPANDED SPACES: FREE APP FOR DOWNLOAD

 Um diese Ausgabe nicht nur gedruckt, sondern auch im digitalen Raum erleben zu können, geben wir Ihnen überall, wo Sie das ayscan-Zeichen sehen, die Möglichkeit, Filme zu betrachten oder in virtuelle Rundgänge einzutauchen und die gedruckten Bilder damit um die Dimension der Bewegung zu erweitern. Laden Sie sich im App Store oder im Google Play Store ganz einfach die ayscan-App kostenlos herunter, scannen Sie mit Ihrem mobilen Endgerät die ganze Buchseite ein und kommen Sie in den umfangreichen Genuss von Bild, Film und Ton. Viel Spaß!

We want you to experience this edition both in print and digitally. Wherever you see the ayscan symbol, we offer you the possibility to watch films or to immerse yourselves in virtual tours, thus adding the dimension of movement to the printed images. Simply download the ayscan app from the App Store or the Google Play Store free of charge, use your mobile end device to scan the entire page of the book and enjoy a whole package of additional photos, films and sounds. Have fun!

INTRODUCTION

RE-USE IN RETAIL

DR. JONS MESSEDAT

Ob bei der Transformation ganzer Stadtquartiere oder der Revitalisierung einzelner Kaufhäuser: Das „Weiterbauen" bestehender Substanz wird in der Retail-Branche zunehmend relevant. Konzepte, die auf eine behutsame Nachnutzung von Flächen, Bauten und Materialien setzen, erhalten bereits verbaute „graue" Energie und leisten einen Beitrag zur Ressourcenschonung. So kann das Urban-Mining-Prinzip, das dem Grundgedanken der Circular Economy folgt, zu einem Impulsgeber für kreislauffähiges Retail Design werden.

Reduce, Re-use, Recycle

Der Dreiklang „Reduce, Re-use, Recycle", zu Deutsch: Reduzieren, Weiterverwenden und Wiederverwerten, steht für die drei Säulen der nachhaltigen Kreislaufwirtschaft. Die drei Rs gelten sowohl für statische Gebäudestrukturen als auch für sämtliche Ausbauelemente, die im Einzelhandel stets einem dynamischen Veränderungsprozess unterliegen. Ursprünglich aus der Abfallwirtschaft kommend, wurde der Slogan bereits 2012 zum Motto des Deutschen Pavillons auf der 13. Internationalen Architekturausstellung La Biennale di Venezia. Noch einen Schritt weiter ging der deutsche Beitrag „Open for Maintenance" 2023, der sich den Themen der Pflege, Reparatur und Instandhaltung im Bauwesen widmete. Den Mittelpunkt bildete eine Materialbörse aus Hinterlassenschaften der vergangenen Ausstellungen, die von der Kuratorenschaft gesammelt, inventarisiert und neu inszeniert wurden. Dazu Bundesbauministerin Klara Geywitz: „Die Ausstellung ‚Wegen Umbau geöffnet' beleuchtet auf anschauliche Weise die aktuellen Herausforderungen im Bauwesen. Zirkuläres Wirtschaften und Urban Mining sind längst keine Spartenthemen mehr. Die Wiederverwertung von Bauteilen muss so normal werden wie das Pfandsystem oder Second-Hand-Kleidung."

Whether it is the transformation of an entire city district or the revitalisation of a single department store: The practice of building on or reusing the existing fabric of buildings is becoming increasingly important in the retail sector. Concepts that focus on the careful reuse of land, buildings and materials preserve grey energy that has already been used in the building process and contribute to the conservation of resources. In this way, the urban mining principle, which follows the basic idea of the circular economy, can become a driving force for circular retail design.

Reduce, re-use, recycle

This triad of terms are the three pillars of the sustainable circular economy. The three 'R's apply both to static building structures and to all fit-out elements, which are always subject to a dynamic process of change in retailing. Originally from the waste management sector, the slogan became the motto of the German Pavilion at the 13th International Architecture Exhibition La Biennale di Venezia back in 2012. The German contribution "Open for Maintenance" in 2023, which was dedicated to the topics of care, repair and maintenance in the construction industry, went a step further. The focal point was an exchange of materials from the leftovers of past exhibitions, which were collected, inventoried and restaged by the curators. Federal Building Minister Klara Geywitz commented: "The exhibition 'Open for Maintenance' vividly illustrates the current challenges in the construction industry. Circular economy and urban mining are no longer niche topics. The recycling of building blocks must become as normal as the bottle deposit system or second-hand clothing."

Reduce: „less is enough"

Die Forderung nach einer Konzentration auf das Wesentliche im Sinne eines „Weniger ist mehr" zielte in der Vergangenheit auf einen puristischen Gestaltungskanon ab. In Zukunft rückt die Forderung nach einem „Mehr" an Reduktion ganz an den Anfang der Wertschöpfungskette. Mit intelligenten Planungstools und nutzergerechten Bedarfsanalysen lässt sich noch vor Beginn des eigentlichen Planungs- und Gestaltungsprozesses maximale Effizienz mit minimalem Verbrauch abgleichen. „Reduce to the max" war das eingängige Motto eines ursprünglich visionären Kleinstwagenkonzepts. Im Kontext des Bauens lässt sich dieser Leitgedanke auf die Reduzierung des Pro-Kopf-Flächenbedarfs sowie die Minimierung des Material-und Ressourcenverbrauchs übertragen. Neben den „harten" Fakten zur Flächen-, Energie- und Kosteneffizienz spielen auch „weiche", nicht unmittelbar in Zahlen messbare Werte eine Rolle: Orte des Handels bieten von jeher Raum für realen sozialen Austausch und die Kommunikation zwischen Generationen und Kulturen. Vor allem dann, wenn vielfältige Nutzungen sich komprimiert überlagern und dadurch hybride Schnittstellen entstehen. Während bei dem bisherigen Streben nach Effizienz eine Verringerung des Inputs bei gleichem Output im Vordergrund stand, hinterfragen neuere Suffizienzstrategien die Notwendigkeit von mehr Wachstum und Konsum im Sinne von „weniger ist genug".

Re-use: „linear wird zirkulär"

In linearen Materialzyklen folgt der Rohstoffgewinnung die Verarbeitung zu speziellen Baustoffen und schließlich der Einsatz vor Ort, auf der Baustelle. Je nach Nutzungsdauer werden die daraus entstandenen Gebäudehüllen und Innenausbauten zurückgebaut und im Idealfall in neuen Projekten weiterverwendet. Für zu viele Materialien folgt aber immer noch die sogenannte „thermische Verwertung", sprich Verbrennung, oder die Deponie als Schlusspunkt der Linie nach dem Motto: „make, take, waste". Die Anforderung an Retail Design als Teil eines zirkulären Prozesses bedeutet hingegen, dies gemäß dem ersten Schritt „Reduce" zu verringern, um möglichst viele „Halbzeuge" in der Wertschöpfungskette zu behalten. In der Praxis scheitert die sinnvolle Weiterverwendung aber meist an der fehlenden Logistik zum Separieren, Transportieren und Einlagern von allgemeinen Baustoffen und speziellen Bauteilen. Vor diesem Hintergrund erschließt sich auch der Appell, der von Architekturbiennale 2023 ausging. Um den Materialfluss nachhaltig „rund" zu bekommen, ist es notwendig, Netzwerke und Handelsplätze sowie Materialkataster mit detaillierten Angaben zu allen verbauten Elementen zu etablieren. Viele Bauteile und Komponenten, von der Haustechnik über Wand-, Boden- und Deckenverkleidungen bis hin zu Präsentationelementen aus dem Shopdesign, können auf diesem Wege einem „Second Life" zugeführt werden.

Reduce: less is enough

In the past, the call for a focus on the essentials in the sense of "less is more" was aimed at a purist design canon. In future, it will place the demand for "more" reduction at the very beginning of the value chain. With intelligent planning tools and user-orientated needs analyses, maximum efficiency can be balanced with minimum consumption even before the actual planning and design process begins. "Reduce to the max" was the catchy motto of an originally visionary compact car concept. In the context of construction, this guiding principle can be applied to the reduction of per capita space requirements and the minimisation of material and resource consumption. In addition to the hard facts about space, energy and cost efficiency, soft values that cannot be directly measured in figures also play a role. Places of commerce have always offered space for real social exchange and communication between generations and cultures. This is especially true when many different uses overlap in a compressed form, creating hybrid interfaces. While the previous pursuit of efficiency focused on reducing input for the same output, more recent sufficiency strategies question the need for more growth and consumption in the sense of "less is enough".

Re-use: linear becomes circular

In linear material cycles, the extraction of raw materials is followed by their processing into special building materials and finally their use on the construction site. Depending on their useful life, the resulting building shells and interior fittings are dismantled and ideally reused in new projects. But for too many materials, the end of the line is still thermal recycling, i.e. incineration, or the landfill true to the motto: make, take, waste. For retail design as part of a circular process, on the other hand, reduction is about keeping as many semi-finished products as possible in the value chain. In practice, however, re-use usually fails due to the lack of logistics for separating, transporting and storing general building materials and special components. Against this background, the meaning of the appeal made by the Architecture Biennale 2023 becomes clear. In order to make the material flow go "round" in the long term, it is necessary to establish networks and trading centres as well as material registers with detailed information on all built elements. In this way, many parts and components, from building services to wall, floor and ceiling cladding to presentation elements from store design, can be given a second life.

Recycle: „upgrading not downgrading"

Um ein stetiges „Downgrading" im Recyclingprozess zu vermeiden, bietet eine „sortenreine" Erfassung aller raumbildenden Elemente vor allem im Ladenbau und Retail Design großes Potenzial. Grundlage dafür ist eine transparente und leicht verständliche Kennzeichnung aller genutzten Ressourcen. Ein Lösungsansatz für diese Forderung ist das Etablieren eines Materialpasses. Ähnlich wie der klassische „Waschzettel" bei Textilien gibt dieser Auskunft zum Ursprung, zur Zusammensetzung und schließlich zum Recycling. So lässt sich vor allem bei Verbundmaterialien der Verlust an Qualität und Wert im Wiederverwertungszyklus minimieren.

Nach dem bereits etablierten Energieausweis, der sich speziell auf die Energieeffizienz und den Energieverbrauch konzentriert, setzt die Idee eines Ressourcenpasses neue Impulse: Dieser soll einen Beitrag zur Transparenz über die verbauten Materialien, die Treibhausgasemissionen von Gebäuden sowie deren Kreislauffähigkeit leisten. Neben den Aktivitäten des Bauministeriums zur Konzeption eines Gesamtansatzes haben verschiedene Akteure, wie die Deutsche Gesellschaft für Nachhaltiges Bauen (DGNB) oder die EPEA GmbH – Part of Drees & Sommer, erste Lösungsansätze für die Bauwirtschaft erarbeitet. Ein weniger greifbarer Baustein findet in den verästelten Regelwerken und Zertifizierungen zur Nachhaltigkeit aber keine Beachtung: Wie nachhaltig ist die Architektur an sich? Ist die Gestaltung auch nach wenigen Jahrzehnten noch „ansehnlich" und flexibel für neue Inhalte?

Precycle: „regenerativ und resilient"

Um die drei Rs nachhaltig umzusetzen, ist es sinnvoll, diese möglichst früh als Eckpunkte im Projektablauf zu fixieren. Ganz zu Anfang sorgen digitalisierte Prozesse wie das BIM-Verfahren (Akronym für „Building Information Modeling") für detaillierte, allen Planungsbeteiligten zugängliche Informationen. So kann ein „digitaler Zwilling" des Projekts erstellt werden, anhand dessen alle verwendeten Ressourcen, Materialien und Produkte gekennzeichnet und lokalisiert sind.

Zu den „Precycling"-Strategien gehören auch klimaresiliente Ansätze, die zu einem reduzierten Wartungsaufwand und Energieverbrauch führen. Noch bedeutet das vorausschauende „Precycling" einen Mehraufwand. Es greift bei Neubauvorhaben wie Supermärkten auf der grünen Wiese und modularen Filialen eher als bei bestehenden, über Jahrzehnte gewachsenen Kaufhauskomplexen in den Innenstädten. Der nicht unerhebliche Aufwand für die Erfassung aller Bauteile, von der einzelnen Schraube bis zu ganzen Innenausbauten, schlägt sich nicht in den Leistungsbildern und Honoraren der Planenden nieder. Zudem sind die verschiedenen Nachhaltigkeitszertifizierungen mit großem Aufwand

Recycle: upgrading not downgrading

In order to avoid constant downgrading in the recycling process, there is great potential in the collection of all space-creating elements in groups of identical materials, especially in shop and retail design. The basis for this is transparent and easy-to-understand labelling of all resources used. One possible solution is the establishment of a material passport. Like the classic care tag for textiles, it provides information on the origin, composition and ultimately recycling. This minimises the loss of quality and value in the recycling cycle, especially for composite materials.

Following the already established energy performance certificate, which focuses specifically on energy efficiency and energy consumption, the idea of a material passport provides a new impetus to create transparency about the materials used, the greenhouse gas emissions of buildings and their recyclability. In addition to the activities of the Ministry of Construction to design an overall approach, various players, such as the German Sustainable Building Council (DGNB) and EPEA GmbH – Part of Drees & Sommer, have developed initial solutions for the construction industry. However, one less tangible component is not taken into account in the complex sets of regulations and certifications for sustainability: How sustainable is the architecture per se? Is the design still "presentable" and flexible enough for new content even after a few decades?

Pre-cycle: regenerative and resilient

In order to implement the three 'R's sustainably, it makes sense to establish them as cornerstones in the project process as early as possible. At the very beginning, digitalised processes such as the BIM process (acronym for Building Information Modelling) provide detailed information that is accessible to all planning participants. This creates a "digital twin" of the project which can be used to identify and locate all resources, materials and products used.

The pre-cycling strategies also include climate-resilient approaches that lead to reduced maintenance and energy consumption. The forward-looking pre-cycling still means extra effort and expense. It is more likely to apply to new construction projects such as supermarkets on greenfield sites and modular stores than to existing department store complexes in city centres that have grown over decades. The not inconsiderable effort involved in recording all components, from individual screws to entire interior fittings, is not reflected in the work profiles and fees of the designers. In addition, the various sustainability certifications involve a great deal of effort and expense. In the long term, however, added value is created in terms of sustainability reporting,

INTRODUCTION

und Kosten verbunden. Langfristig wird aber ein Mehrwert im Sinne des Nachhaltigkeitsreportings geschaffen, das in der ESG-Transformation (Environmental, Social, Governance) und mit den Forderungen der EU-Taxonomie an Bedeutung gewinnt.

Retail Transformation

Frequentierte Orte des Handels sorgen für Vitalität, Vielfalt und Sicherheit in unseren Innenstädten. Wie bestehende Strukturen mit neuem Leben gefüllt werden, beschreibt Architekt MSc. ETH Albert Achammer im Interview „Leerstand ist Stillstand". Mit der Initiative „New Life –Neues Leben für Warenhäuser" engagiert er sich für neue Lebensqualität in den europäischen Innenstädten. Dass Verantwortung gegenüber der Umwelt integraler Bestandteil einer erfolgreichen (Retail-)Architektur sein muss und wie diese in interdisziplinär arbeitenden Teams umgesetzt wird, zeigt Innenarchitektin Jutta Blocher in ihrem Beitrag „Vernetzt Denken, zukunftsfähig Bauen". Perspektiven für die Zukunft des Einzelhandels testet die Rid Stiftung mit dem Förderformat Future Retail Store. Die Erkenntnisse daraus werden mit dem Führungsnachwuchs, Kommunen und Forschung geteilt, um die Zukunft von Stadt und Handel gemeinsam gestalten zu können.

Zu den sechs vom Deutschen Bundeskabinett forcierten Transformationsbereichen mit dringendem Handlungsbedarf zählen die Schwerpunkte Klimaschutz, Kreislaufwirtschaft und Nachhaltiges Bauen. Diese Aspekte werden einem regelmäßigen Monitoring unterzogen und einmal pro Legislaturperiode fortgeschrieben. „Die bisherigen Erfahrungen mit der Umsetzung der Agenda 2030 national wie global zeigen: Wir können nachhaltiger werden. Zugleich wird klar: Wir müssen noch sehr viel tun und vor allem aufs Tempo drücken, denn 2030 ist bereits in Sicht!", heißt es in der Deutschen Nachhaltigkeitsstrategie. Ein enges Zeitfenster mit weiten Perspektiven für kreatives und intelligentes Retail Design! Ich freue mich über die Bandbreite der eingereichten Projekte, die, von der wiederverwendbaren Brand Box über erlebnisreiche Stores bis hin zu erfolgreich revitalisierten Kaufhäusern, alle für mehr Lebensqualität in unseren Innenstädten sorgen.

which is becoming increasingly important in the ESG (Environmental, Social, Governance) transformation and with the requirements of the EU taxonomy.

Retail transformation

Busy retail locations with a high footfall ensure vitality, diversity and safety in our city centres. How existing structures are filled with new life is described by architect MSc. ETH Albert Achammer in the interview "Vacancy means standstill". With the "New Life for Department Stores" initiative, he is committed to a new quality of life in European city centres. In her article "A networked approach to building for the future", interior designer Jutta Blocher argues that responsibility towards the environment must be an integral part of successful (retail) architecture and explains how this is implemented in interdisciplinary teams. The Rid Foundation is testing perspectives for the future of retail with the Future Retail Store funding format. The findings are shared with experts from retail, urban development and research to co-shape the future of cities and retailing.

The six transformation areas with an urgent need for action promoted by the German Federal Cabinet include climate protection, the circular economy and sustainable construction. These aspects are subject to regular monitoring and are updated once per legislative period. "Experience with the implementation of the 2030 Agenda both nationally and globally has so far shown that we can become more sustainable. At the same time, one thing is clear: There is still a lot to be done and, above all, we need to speed up because 2030 is already in sight," says the German sustainability strategy. A narrow window of opportunity with broad perspectives for creative and intelligent retail design! I am delighted with the range of projects submitted, from the reusable brand box and themed stores through to successfully revitalised department stores, all of which contribute to a better quality of life in our city centres.

VACANCY MEANS STANDSTILL
CITY STRUCTURE: HOW DO WE NOW SUSTAINABLY REBUILD OUR CITY CENTRES?

ALBERT ACHAMMER, ATP ARCHITEKTEN INGENIEURE

Mit der Initiative „New Life – Neues Leben für Warenhäuser" haben Sie einen Diskurs gegen Leer- und Stillstand in unseren Innenstädten initiiert. Wie gehen Sie dabei vor und wie ist das bisherige Echo?

Viele Architekt:innen sind durch ihre Ausbildung oft dem Objekt, also dem Gebäude, viel näher, als sie es seiner Umgebung sind. Und trotzdem ist es der „Negativraum", also der Raum zwischen den Gebäuden, in dem die Öffentlichkeit sich aus unterschiedlichsten Anlässen begegnet. Gebäude tragen unserer Meinung nach eine große Verantwortung, diesen öffentlichen Raum zu bespielen und zu beleben. Dabei gibt es Akteure im städtischen Kontext mit unterschiedlicher Dominanz.

Wir sind als Netzwerkorganisation fest davon überzeugt, dass man Herausforderungen ab einer gewissen Größe und Wichtigkeit nicht mehr allein, sondern nur noch im Kollektiv bewältigen kann. Dies ganz im Sinne unseres zentralen Unternehmenswerts: Zusammenarbeit. Deshalb haben wir die Fühler ausgestreckt und nach Mitstreitern gesucht, denen die Qualität der europäischen Innenstadt genauso am Herzen liegt wie uns. Wir sind mit informellen Gesprächen gestartet, die wir dann in einem Positionspapier (Whitepaper) veröffentlichen. Darauf aufbauend haben wir eine Reihe an Diskussionsrunden mit sehr diversem Teilnehmerkreis initiiert. Die gute und intensive Resonanz hat uns nur in unserer Annahme bestätigt, dass es kein rein städtebauliches, architektonisches oder betriebswirtschaftliches Thema ist, sondern Teil des gesellschaftlichen Lebens, das uns in vielen Dimensionen berührt.

With the "New Life for Department Stores" initiative, you have started a discourse against vacancies and stagnation in our city centres. How did you go about it and what has the response been so far?

Because of their training, many architects are often much closer to the building than they are to its surroundings. And yet it is in the 'negative space', i.e. the space between the buildings, that the public meets on many different occasions. We believe that buildings have a great responsibility to bring this public space to life. There are actors in the urban context with varying degrees of dominance.

As a network organisation, we firmly believe that challenges of a certain scale and importance can no longer be tackled alone, but only collectively. This is entirely in line with our core corporate value of collaboration. That's why we put out our feelers, looking for fellow campaigners who care about the quality of the Europe's city centres as much as we do. We started with informal discussions, which we then published in a white paper setting out our position. Building on this, we initiated a series of discussions with a very diverse group of participants. The positive and intense response has only confirmed our assumption that this is not a purely urban planning, architectural or economic issue, but a part of the fabric of society that affects us in many dimensions.

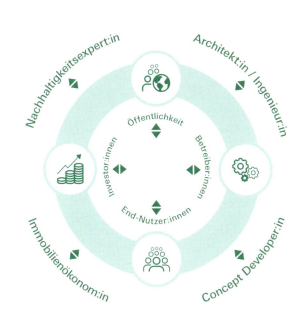

Interdisziplinäre Zusammenarbeit eröffnet neue Perspektiven für Warenhausimmobilien.
Interdisciplinary cooperation opens up new perspectives for retail properties.

Viele Kaufhäuser in den Innenstädten und auch Einkaufszentren in der Peripherie sind mittlerweile in die Jahre gekommen. Kann durch Revitalisierung statt Abriss ein wirtschaftlicher und städtebaulicher Mehrwert generiert werden?

Diese Frage kann man nicht pauschal beantworten, da jedes Gebäude in seinem eigenen Kontext gesehen werden muss. Es gibt durchaus Orte, wo sowohl Warenhäuser als auch Shoppingcenter weiterhin einen wirtschaftlichen und gesellschaftlichen Mehrwert leisten können. Mit einem klugen Repositioning oder einer gelungenen Revitalisierung werden diese Gebäude einen positiv nachhaltigen Effekt für diese Kommunen erwirken. Die wirklich guten Center wurden als Imitation einer europäischen Innenstadt konzipiert mit imitierten Plätzen, Sichtachsen, Stadtbalkonen usw., die zum Verweilen über den ganzen Tag animieren. Für viele neue Stadtentwicklungen, denen diese Dichte, auch aufgrund städtebaulicher Fehlentwicklungen, fehlt, dienen diese Einkaufszentren noch heute als Innenstadtersatz. Solange solche Zentren diesen gesellschaftlichen Mehrwert bieten können, wird es für sie auch eine Zukunft geben.

Das innerstädtische Kaufhaus war als großes Verkaufslager mit einem Betreiber (etwa Hertie, Karstadt, Kaufhof) konzipiert. Dieses exklusiv auf Kauf ausgerichtete Geschäftsmodell funktioniert seit vielen Jahren nicht mehr, denn die kommunikativen Bedürfnisse der Endnutzer (Kunden) haben sich schon lange verändert. Das Warenhaus der Nachkriegszeit hat allerdings ein paar entscheidende Vorteile, selbst wenn die Nutzung, die Programmierung nicht mehr funktioniert. So erlaubt die robuste Gebäudestruktur zumeist eine Vielzahl an unterschiedlichen Nutzungen. Auch die Lage birgt ein erhebliches Potenzial, um diese „Black Boxes" wieder in die Innenstädte einzugliedern und damit Städten und Gemeinden neue Impulse zu geben.

Many department stores in city centres and shopping centres on the outskirts are getting on in years. Can revitalisation, rather than demolition, add value to the economy and urban development?

There is no general answer to this question, as each building has to be seen in its own context. There are certainly places where both department stores and shopping centres can continue to add economic and social value. With clever repositioning or successful revitalisation, these buildings will have a positive, sustainable impact on these communities. The really good shopping centres were designed to imitate a European city centre with imitation squares, visual axes, city balconies, etc. that encourage people to linger throughout the day. For many new urban developments that lack this density, partly due to urban planning mistakes, these shopping centres still serve as a substitute for city centres today. As long as such centres can offer this social added value, they will have a future.

The inner-city department store was conceived as a large retail warehouse with one operator (e.g. Hertie, Karstadt, Kaufhof). This exclusively purchase-orientated business model has not worked for many years, as the communicative needs of end users (customers) have long since changed. However, the department store of the post-war era has a few decisive advantages, even if the use, i.e. their programming, no longer works. The robust building structure usually allows a variety of different uses. The location also offers considerable potential to reintegrate these 'black boxes' into city centres and thus give new impetus to cities and communities.

Um strategische Partnerschaften zwischen Investoren, Kommunen und Betreibern zu schließen, sind Engagement und Ideen notwendig. Aus welcher Richtung kommen da aus ihrer Sicht innovative Impulse?

Ich bin deshalb ein so großer Freund von Kollaboration, weil Innovation nach meiner Erfahrung immer aus der Kombination von schon Bekanntem entsteht. Vielversprechende Ansätze gibt es auch heute bereits viele. Diese reichen von modernen Betreiberkonzepten bis hin zu effizienten baulichen Lösungen. Die wahre Innovation entsteht aber in der Kombination dieser Impulse zu zukunftsfähigen Lösungen – maßgeschneidert auf jeden spezifischen Fall. Dafür benötigt es ein Zusammenspiel von Spezialisten und Generalisten.

Vakante Orte wie leer stehende Kauf- und Parkhäuser bieten viel Raum für neue Nutzungen aus ganz unterschiedlichen Bereichen. Welche synergetischen Kombinationen können Sie sich unter einem Dach vorstellen?

Natürlich können sich durch die Kombination von Nutzungen im Gebäude Synergien ergeben. Weil die Gebäude normalerweise sehr groß sind, finden solche Synergien auf vielen Ebenen statt. Das reicht von der kontinuierlichen Belebung der Flächen über einen Tagesverlauf bis hin zu sich ergänzenden haustechnischen Systemen. Trotzdem würde ich hier gern über das einzelne Dach hinausdenken. Wir haben in unseren Städten unterschiedlich große und unterschiedlich frequentierte Stadtbausteine. Ein Quartier lebt davon, dass unterschiedliche Nutzungen in einem fußläufigen Radius von 15 bis 20 Minuten erreichbar sind. Nicht jedes Gebäude hat die Möglichkeit, in seiner Struktur diverse Bruchteile der Quartiersfunktion abzubilden. Das ist auch gar nicht nötig, denn es gibt bestimmte Stadtbausteine, die größere und öffentliche Funktionen wunderbar übernehmen können, wie Kirchen, Rathäuser usw. Diese könnten zukünftig sehr gut durch den Stadtbaustein „neues Warenhaus" ergänzt werden.

Nach dem Auszug der ursprünglichen Mieter folgen oft befristete Pop-up-Formate, um den Leerstand zu kaschieren. Sind das eher preiswerte „Pausenfüller" oder können Sie sich vorstellen, dass in Zukunft mehr temporäre Nutzungen gefragt sind?

Ich denke, man kann dieses Urteil noch nicht endgültig fällen. Es gibt einige Pop-ups, die durchaus Potenzial haben. Vor allem um für manche Akteure einen weiteren, anderen Vermarktungskanal zu eröffnen und auch um on- mit offline zu verbinden. Die Experimente der letzten Jahre liefen allerdings – auch aufgrund einer schwierigen Marktlage – wirtschaftlich noch nicht ideal, zumindest solange man sie für sich allein betrachtet.

Commitment and ideas are needed to forge strategic partnerships between investors, municipalities and operators. Where do you see innovative impetus coming from?

I am such a big fan of collaboration because, in my experience, innovation always comes from combining what is already known. There are already many promising approaches ranging from modern operator concepts to efficient structural solutions. However, the real innovation comes from combining these impulses to create future-proof solutions – tailored to each specific case. This requires interaction between specialists and generalists.

Vacant locations such as empty department stores and parking garages offer plenty of space for new uses in very different areas. What synergetic combinations can you imagine under one roof?

Synergies can result from the combination of uses in the building. Because the buildings are usually very large, such synergies take place on many levels. This ranges from the continuous animation of the areas over the course of a day to complementary building services systems. Nevertheless, I would like to think beyond the single roof. In our cities, we have different sized and differently frequented urban building blocks. A neighbourhood thrives on different uses being within a walking radius of 15 to 20 minutes. Not every building has the possibility to map diverse fractions of the neighbourhood function in its structure. Nor is this necessary, as there are certain urban building blocks that can take on larger and public functions wonderfully, such as churches, town halls, etc. These could very well be supplemented in future by the 'new department store' urban building block.

After the original tenants move out, temporary pop-up formats often follow to conceal the vacancy. Are these just inexpensive 'stop gaps', or can you imagine that temporary uses will be more in demand in future?

I don't think it is possible to make a final judgment just yet. There are some pop-ups that definitely have potential. Above all to open up another new marketing channel for some players and also to combine online and offline. However, the experiments of recent years have not yet been ideal in economic terms – partly due to the difficult market situation – at least as long as they are considered in isolation.

Entwurf eines multifunktionalen Begegnungszentrums.
Rendering of a multifunctional centre of encounter.

In einer Makro-Betrachtung können diese Zwischennutzungen allerdings enorm wertvoll sein. Denn die Außenraumqualität städtischer Orte ist unglaublich abhängig davon, wie kontinuierlich belebt diese Orte werden. Während eines monate- oder gar jahrelangen Leerstands einer solch großen Immobilie verändert sich auch die Umgebung. Benachbarte Geschäfte büßen Umsätze ein, ganze Straßenzüge können verwaisen und es bilden sich dunkle Ecken, die für die Öffentlichkeit zu Problemzonen werden können. Um solchen Situationen entgegenzuwirken, sind temporäre Zwischennutzungen ideal. Sie haben einen positiven ökonomischen und gesellschaftlichen Effekt auf die Umgebung, auch wenn sie sich möglicherweise selbst nicht tragen. Somit sollten eigentlich viele ein Interesse daran haben, Zwischennutzungen zu ermöglichen.

Der Handel ist der wesentliche Motor für Bewegung und Frequenz in den Städten. Wie muss sich der Handel vor Ort wandeln, um wieder Fahrt aufzunehmen und neue Kundschaft für den Besuch zu begeistern?

Der reine Kauf begeistert fast niemanden und die Notwendigkeit, dafür physisch wohin zu fahren, wird auch immer geringer. Der Onlinehandel hat dafür gesorgt, dass sich unser Konsumverhalten nachhaltig verändert hat. Allerdings kann das Onlineshopping die physische Begegnung (noch) nicht ersetzen. Diese Begegnung, im Zusammenspiel mit guter Beratung, Atmosphäre und tollen Erlebnissen, ist es, was den physischen Handel noch interessant macht. Auch eine ausgewogene Kombination von Angeboten wirkt anziehend. Erfolgreiche Retailer haben dies längst verstanden. Das ist auch der Grund, warum sich vor manchen Geschäften immer noch Schlangen bilden.

From a macro perspective, however, these interim uses can be enormously valuable. The quality of outdoor spaces in urban areas is incredibly dependent on the degree to which these spaces are constantly in use. During months or even years of vacancy of such a large property, the surroundings also change. Neighbouring stores lose sales, entire streets can become deserted and dark corners develop that can become problem areas for the public. Temporary interim uses are ideal for counteracting such situations. They have a positive economic and social impact on the surrounding area, even if they may not be self-sustaining. This means that many people should actually have an interest in enabling temporary use.

Retail is the main driver of movement and footfall in cities. How does local retail need to change in order to regain momentum and attract new customers?

Hardly anyone is enthusiastic about just buying things and the need to go somewhere to do so is on the wane. Online retail has changed our consumer behaviour forever. However, online shopping cannot (yet) replace physical encounters. This encounter, in combination with good advice, atmosphere and great experiences, is what still makes physical retail so interesting. A balanced combination of offers also has an attractive effect. Successful retailers have long understood this. This is also the reason why there are still queues outside some stores.

Großvolumige Gebäude bieten eine Vielzahl an unterschiedlichen Nutzungen.
Large-scale buildings offer a multitude of possible functions.

Welche Retail-Projekte bei ATP und auch darüber hinaus beschäftigen und begeistern Sie derzeit? Gibt es internationale Beispiele und Entwicklungen, die neue Perspektiven für den Handel aufzeigen?

Mich begeistern momentan vor allem jene unserer aktuellen Retail-Projekte, die mit mehr Komplexität zu tun haben als dem reinen Verkaufen von Waren. Ich denke, unsere Städte und auch die Art, wie wir als Menschen interagieren, sind von hoher Komplexität geprägt – das haben wir in den letzten Jahrzehnten vielleicht etwas vernachlässigt. Eines der spannendsten Projekte, an denen wir momentan arbeiten, ist das Überseequartier in Hamburg. Da entsteht ein ganz neuer Stadtteil, im Sockel organisiert wie ein Einkaufszentrum, aber darüber hoch multifunktional mit Wohnen, Hotel, Büro und auch Quartiersfunktionen. Wir bearbeiten das Thema Retail aber oft in viel kleinerem Maßstab, beispielsweise beim Umbau eines kleinen Kaufhauses mitten in Rostock (S. 148) oder bei der Repositionierung von Retailflächen in Basel (S. 156).

Which retail projects at ATP and beyond are currently keeping you busy and inspiring you? Are there international examples and developments that show new perspectives for retail?

At the moment, I am particularly enthusiastic about our current retail projects that involve more complexity than simply selling goods. I think our cities and the way we interact as humans are characterised by a high degree of complexity – we have perhaps neglected this somewhat in recent decades. One of the most exciting projects we are currently working on is the Überseequartier district in Hamburg. A completely new district is being created, organised like a shopping centre at the base, but highly multifunctional above with residential, hotel, office and district functions. However, we often work on the topic of retail on a much smaller scale, for example when converting a small department store in the middle of Rostock (p. 148) or repositioning retail space in Basle (p. 156).

Ich glaube, der Handel hat immer schon davon gelebt, dass Menschen zusammenkommen. Dadurch entstanden in Europa die schönsten Basiliken und die besten Marktplätze. Die neuen Perspektiven sind für mich tatsächlich nicht neu: nämlich die Grundlage für ein Erlebnis zu schaffen. Natürlich müssen dabei neue Technologien, Demografien usw. berücksichtigt werden, aber das Grundrezept hat sich nicht verändert. Alle erfolgreichen Projekte, die wir in der Vergangenheit und Gegenwart betreut haben und betreuen, erfüllen diese Vorgabe.

Zu Ihren Erinnerungen gehört das gemeinsame familiäre Flanieren am Wochenende. Welche Zutaten wünschen Sie sich, um diese Tradition in Zukunft auch mit der nächsten Generation zu teilen?

Ich bin davon überzeugt, dass Städte wieder mehr in ihren eigenen, spezifischen Charakter investieren müssen. Die europäischen Innenstädte sind Orte, für die uns der Rest der Welt beneidet. Sie bieten unglaubliche Qualitäten, die man teilweise nur wieder etwas besser in Szene setzen muss. Ich glaube, die Menschen sehnen sich nach Gemeinschaft, nach Austausch und Begegnung und unsere Innenstädte bieten die idealen Voraussetzungen dafür. Mit der richtigen Programmierung und dem richtigen, individuellen und nicht generischen Charakter jeder einzelnen unserer Städte benötigt es gar nicht so viele neue Zutaten. Ich jedenfalls werde weiterhin großartige Städte zu Fuß entdecken und genießen und denke, dass auch die nächste Generation damit nicht brechen wird.

I believe that retail has always thrived on people coming together. This gave rise to the most beautiful basilicas and the best market squares in Europe. The new perspectives are not new to me; they create the basis for an experience. Of course, new technologies, demographics, etc. have to be taken into account, but the basic recipe has not changed. All of the successful projects that we have managed in the past and are currently managing fulfil this requirement.

Your memories include strolling around together as a family at the weekend. What ingredients would you like to see in order to share this tradition with the next generation in future?

I am convinced that cities need to invest more in their own specific character again. European city centres are the envy of the rest of the world. They offer incredible qualities, some of which just need to be showcased a little better. I believe that people long for community, exchange and encounters, and our city centres offer the ideal conditions for this. With the right programming and the right, individual and non-generic character of each of our cities, it won't take that many new ingredients. I, for one, will continue to discover and enjoy great cities on foot and I don't think the next generation will break with that either.

Mit 1.700+ Mitarbeitenden an derzeit 14 Standorten in DACH und CEE plant die ATP-Gruppe für Auftraggeber aus Forschung, Industrie, Handel, Immobilienwirtschaft und Gesundheitswesen, unterstützt durch eigene Forschungs-, Sonderplanungs- und Consulting-Gesellschaften. Dabei nutzt ATP die „Corporate Structure", um sich als lernende Organisation permanent weiterzuentwickeln. Auf der Basis von 45 Jahren gelebter integraler Planungskultur hat ATP die Organisation und die dazugehörigen Prozesse so gestaltet, dass ideale Voraussetzungen für einen digitalisierten Planungsprozess gegeben sind. Bereits seit 2012 plant ATP durchgehend mit BIM.
www.atp.ag

With more than 1,700 employees at currently 14 locations in German-speaking countries and CEE, the ATP Group designs for clients in research, industry, retail, real estate and healthcare, supported by its own research, specialist design and consulting companies. ATP uses its corporate structure to develop continuously as a learning organisation. Based on 45 years of integral design culture, ATP has structured the organisation and the associated processes in such a way that ideal conditions are in place for a digitalised design process. ATP has been using Building Information Modelling (BIM) for integrated design since 2012.
www.atp.ag

A NETWORKED APPROACH TO BUILDING FOR THE FUTURE

JUTTA BLOCHER, BLOCHER PARTNERS

Nachhaltigkeit ist längst kein Trend mehr, sondern eine Notwendigkeit im modernen Bauwesen. Unternehmen wie blocher partners beweisen, dass transdisziplinäre, ko-kreative Lösungen oft besonders innovativ sind – und dass Verantwortung gegenüber der Umwelt integraler Bestandteil einer erfolgreichen (Retail-)Architektur sein muss.

Das Global Footprint Network errechnet seit Jahrzehnten den Erdüberlastungstag. Zurzeit fällt dieser auf Anfang August. Das bedeutet, nach sieben Monaten sind die Ressourcen, die für zwölf Monate reichen sollten, aufgebraucht. Würden alle Menschen so wirtschaften wie wir in Deutschland, fiele dieser Tag 2024 auf den 2. Mai, womit wir im europäischen Mittelfeld liegen. Das ist schlicht und ergreifend zu früh: Acht Monate im Jahr leben wir auf Pump des Planeten, gerade für uns sparsame Schwaben ein nicht zu tolerierender Missstand.

Die Forderung nach einer Bauwende ist daher in aller Munde – folgerichtig hat die Bundesregierung ein eigenes Ministerium für das Bauen eingerichtet. Klara Geywitz versprach bei Amtsantritt, es würden 400.000 neue Wohnungen im Jahr entstehen. Für nachhaltiges Bauen ist dieses Versprechen tückisch, denn es ist rein quantitativ. Wir müssen nicht einfach viele Häuser bauen, sondern nachhaltigere Häuser, die länger leben: weil sie vielfältig nutzbar sind, erweiterbar, materiell sowie ästhetisch langlebig und im Zweifel leicht rückbau- und rezyklierfähig. Wenn heute einem Gebäude eine Lebensdauer von 30 bis 40 Jahren zugebilligt wird, dann muss unser Ziel sein, diese Dauer zu verdrei-, ja zu verzehnfachen.

Sustainability is no longer just a trend in the building sector. It has become a necessity in modern construction. Companies like blocher partners demonstrate that transdisciplinary, co-creative solutions are often the most innovative – and that environmental responsibility must be an integral part of successful (retail) architecture.

The Global Footprint Network has been calculating the Earth Overshoot Day for decades. It currently falls at the beginning of August. This means that after seven months, the resources that should last for twelve months are used up. If everyone did business the way we do in Germany, this day would have fallen on 2 May in 2024, which would put us in the middle of the European field. That is simply too early: For eight months of the year we live on the planet's credit, an intolerable state of affairs, especially for us thrifty Swabians.

Everyone is calling for a turnaround in the construction industry, and the German government has even set up a separate ministry for construction. When Klara Geywitz took office, she promised that 400,000 new homes would be built every year. In terms of sustainable construction this purely quantitative goal is risky. We don't just need to build more houses, what we need are more sustainable houses that last longer: because they are versatile, extendable, durable in both material and aesthetic terms and, if the worst comes to the worst, can be easily dismantled and recycled. If a building is currently expected to last 30 to 40 years, then our goal must be to extend this period by three or even ten times.

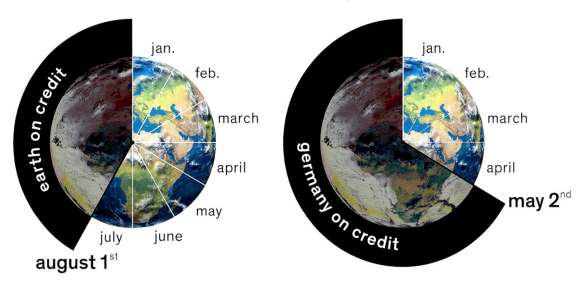

Earth Overshoot Day: Fünf Monate im Jahr leben die Menschen auf Kosten nachfolgender Generationen, die Deutschen sogar acht Monate im Jahr.
Earth Overshoot Day: Five months of the year people live at the expense of future generations, in Germany even eight months of the year.

Bauen im Bestand, Ideen mit Bestand

Ressourcenschonende Prozesse – dazu zählen wir auch die Bestandserhaltung – gehören schon immer zu unserem beruflichen Alltag. Doch der Klimawandel stellt das Bauwesen und damit auch Architekturunternehmen vor weitaus größere globale Herausforderungen. Das heißt, wir müssen Stadtentwicklung neu denken, denn wir wollen nicht nur umweltschonende Lösungen entwickeln, sondern gleichzeitig sollen sie ästhetisch ansprechend und funktional sein. Bauen auf der grünen Wiese ist keine Option mehr, stattdessen müssen wir bestehende Strukturen möglichst nachverdichten und obsolete Gebäude einem neuen Zweck zuführen. Auch sperrige Immobilien bergen Chancen für neue Nutzung: Zu besichtigen ist das etwa beim Haus der Statistik in Berlin, das durch Umbau neben Büros der öffentlichen Verwaltung auch Wohnungen und Künstlerateliers erhalten wird (siehe auch Wollhaus in Heilbronn, S. 160).

Wir müssen uns immer wieder vor Augen führen, dass, wenn wir von Nachhaltigkeit sprechen, auf unseren Schultern eine enorme Hypothek lastet. Rufen wir uns noch einmal die Fakten ins Gedächtnis: Die Bauwirtschaft ist weltweit verantwortlich für ungefähr 40 Prozent des Energieverbrauchs, 50 Prozent der Emissionen von klimaschädlichen Gasen, 50 Prozent des Abfallaufkommens, 60 Prozent des Ressourcenverbrauchs und 70 Prozent des Flächenverbrauchs (Zahlen aus Vittorio Magnago Lampugnani: *Gegen Wegwerfarchitektur*, Berlin 2023, S. 7). Wie also den ökologischen Fußabdruck reduzieren, ohne ökonomische und soziale Aspekte zu vernachlässigen?

Existing buildings: rethinking existence

Processes that conserve – including the preservation of existing buildings – have always been part of our everyday work. However, climate change poses a far greater global challenge to the construction industry and therefore to architects. This means we have to rethink urban development, because the solutions we develop should not only be environmentally friendly, but also aesthetically pleasing and functional. Building on greenfield sites is no longer an option; instead, we need to redensify existing structures wherever possible and repurpose obsolete buildings. Even the most bulky properties offer opportunities for new uses. The House of Statistics is a good example. This building in Berlin is to be converted into public administration offices along with apartments and artists' studios (see also Wollhaus in Heilbronn, p. 160).

We must always remember that when we talk about sustainability, we carry a huge burden on our shoulders. Let's look at the facts: The construction industry is responsible for around 40 percent of energy consumption worldwide, 50 percent of greenhouse gas emissions, 50 percent of waste generation, 60 percent of resource consumption and 70 percent of land use (figures from Vittorio Magnago Lampugnani: *Gegen Wegwerfarchitektur*, Berlin 2023, p. 7). So how can we reduce our ecological footprint without neglecting economic and social aspects?

Eine Antwort auf diese Frage gibt das Umwandlungsprojekt „New 7" in Mannheim. Galeria Kaufhof ist 2020 ausgezogen, woraufhin wir mit unserem Auftraggeber Diringer & Scheidel ein Konzept für ein zukunftsfähiges Gebäude entwickelt haben. Wir haben uns dafür entschieden, das Skelett bis zum ersten Obergeschoss zu erhalten, um darauf vier Geschosse in Holzhybridbauweise zu setzen. Die Elemente werden in größtmöglichem Umfang vorproduziert. Damit erreichen wir mehrere Ziele zugleich: Ein substanzieller Teil der grauen Energie wird erhalten, die Bauzeit reduziert sich ungemein, es entsteht eine zukunftsfähige Nutzungsmischung aus Wohnen in den Obergeschossen und aus Büros und Geschäften vom ersten Ober- bis ins Kellergeschoss. Im Herbst 2023 wurde der Umbau begonnen und schon 2025 wird das New 7 fertig sein.

The New 7 conversion project in Mannheim provides an answer to this question. After Galeria Kaufhof moved out in 2020, we worked with our client Diringer & Scheidel to develop a concept for a future-proof building. We decided to retain the skeleton up to the second floor in order to build four storeys on top in hybrid timber construction. By prefabricating the elements to the greatest possible extent, several goals are achieved at the same time: A substantial amount of grey energy is conserved, the construction time is greatly reduced, and a sustainable mix of uses is created, consisting of living in the upper floors and offices and shops from the ground floor to the basement. Conversion work began in autumn 2023 and the New 7 will be completed by 2025.

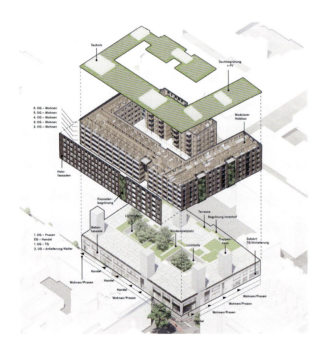

Für das New 7 werden auf das bestehende Betonskelett Geschosse in Holzhybridbauweise gesetzt.
For the New 7, four storeys in hybrid timber construction are built on top of the existing concrete skeleton.

Was früher nur ein Kaufhaus war, wird in Zukunft eine Mischung aus Wohnungen, Büros und Geschäften sein.
What was once only a department store is now going to be a mixture of apartments, offices and stores.

A NETWORKED APPROACH TO BUILDING FOR THE FUTURE

Die vertikale Stadt des Q 6 Q 7: Über der Mall befinden sich Wohnungen und ein Gemeinschaftsgarten.
The vertical city of Q 6 Q 7: Above the mall are apartments and a community garden.

Unter den Wohnungen gelegen: die Mall.
Located beneath the apartments: the mall.

Think through the boxes

Für besonders erfolgversprechend halten wir die Zusammenarbeit von transdisziplinären Teams, eine Praxis, die uns seit Bürogründung 1989 begleitet. Ein Paradebeispiel der jüngeren Vergangenheit ist das gemischt genutzte Stadtquartier „Q 6 Q 7" in Mannheim, das bei der Eröffnung 2016 in der Presse als vertikale Stadt beschrieben wurde. Q 6 Q 7 ist ein urbaner Baustein neuen Typs, der das Leben in den Stadtkern zurückbringt – und das nicht nur zu Geschäftszeiten. Das Gebäude wird rund um die Uhr genutzt, wodurch der Betrieb so energieeffizient wie möglich ist. Viel entscheidender ist jedoch der soziale und kulturelle Gewinn für die Mannheimer Innenstadt: Höhere soziale Kontrolle und geringerer Individualverkehr sind davon nur zwei Aspekte. Wohnen, Arbeiten, kulturelles und soziales Leben in fußläufiger Entfernung und in ästhetisch ansprechendem Gewand – damit wird echte Nachhaltigkeit beschrieben. Genau diese Qualitäten würdigte die DGNB mit der Gold-Zertifizierung. Die Verbindung zwischen gesellschaftlicher Entwicklung und Nachhaltigkeit ist somit wechselseitig. Die beiden Elemente zusammenzudenken ist essenziell, um die Herausforderungen der Zukunft erfolgreich zu meistern und eine lebenswerte Umwelt für kommende Generationen zu sichern.

Think through the boxes

We believe that working in transdisciplinary teams is particularly constructive and have been doing so since the office was founded in 1989. A prime example of this in the recent past is the mixed-use urban district Q 6 Q 7 in Mannheim, which was described in the press as a 'vertical city' when it opened in 2016. Q 6 Q 7 is a new type of urban building block that revitalises the city centre – and not just during business hours. The building is in use around the clock, making its operation as energy-efficient as possible. Much more important, however, is the social and cultural benefit for Mannheim's city centre: Greater social control and less individual traffic are just two aspects of this. Living, working, cultural and social life within walking distance and in an aesthetically pleasing design – that is true sustainability. It was precisely these qualities that the German Sustainable Building Council (DGNB) recognised with the Gold certification. The link between social development and sustainability is therefore a two-way street. Combining these two elements is essential if we are to successfully master the challenges of the future and secure an environment worth living in for future generations.

Der Bründl-Store in Kaprun, von der ÖGNI mit Platin-Siegel ausgezeichnet.
The Bründl store in Kaprun, which ÖGNI awarded the platinum seal.

Darum planen wir in mehreren Schritten: Gemeinsam mit unseren Strategieexperten von blocher partners sens und den Nachhaltigkeitsstrategen von blocher partners sustain stellen wir an den Beginn eines jeden Projekts eine detaillierte Analyse der Bedürfnisse und Anforderungen der zukünftigen Nutzer. Darüber hinaus kann unsere Kommunikationsagentur typenraum den Auftraggeber in Fragen der Kommunikationsstrategie beraten. Nachhaltiges Planen, Bauen und Betreiben beginnt ebenfalls schon bei der Bedarfsermittlung, um Immobilien in eine nachhaltige Zukunft zu führen. Basierend auf den gewonnenen Erkenntnissen setzt erst jetzt, nach dieser Leistungsphase 0, der eigentliche Gestaltungsprozess ein. In ko-kreativer Zusammenarbeit entstehen auf dieser Grundlage nach der BIM-Methodik Konzepte, die ökologische Ansprüche erfüllen sowie funktional und ästhetisch überzeugen. Wichtig ist uns dabei, für zukünftige Veränderungen aufgeschlossen und flexibel zu bleiben. Damit stellen wir sicher, dass unsere Gebäude und Räume auch langfristig den Bedürfnissen der Nutzer entsprechen.

Für den Sportartikelhändler Bründl in den österreichischen Alpen etwa haben wir 2008 den Flagshipstore in Kaprun errichtet und 2021 erweitert. Maßgebend seit dem ersten Pinselstrich auf sämtlichen Ebenen war und ist hier unser Commitment. Unseren Bau, der mit dem österreichischen Staatspreis ausgezeichnet wurde, haben wir respektvoll und doch innovativ fortgeschrieben: Wir wollten ihn noch nachhaltiger machen. Unsere Anstrengungen wurden belohnt, denn die Österreichische Gesellschaft für Nachhaltige Immobilienwirtschaft (ÖGNI) zeichnete uns in den Bereichen Innenausbau und Restaurant mit dem Platin-Siegel aus. Es ist die erste derartige Auszeichnung für Innenräume in Österreich. Ein Erfolg, der gleichermaßen auf die Ambition unseres Kunden, unser Know-how wie auf die erzielten Synergien zurückzuführen ist. Für Bründl übernehmen wir nicht nur Hoch- und Innenausbau, sondern auch die Gestaltung der Leitsysteme und die Kommunikation.

That is why we design in several steps: Together with our strategy experts at blocher partners sens and the sustainability strategists at blocher partners sustain, we start every project with a detailed analysis of the needs and requirements of future users. In addition, our communication agency typenraum is able to offer the client consultation on the topic of communication strategy. Sustainable design, construction and operation also begins with the identification of requirements in order to guide real estate into a sustainable future. Based on the information gathered, it is only now, after this work phase 0, that the actual design process begins. In co-creative collaboration, we use BIM to develop concepts that meet ecological, functional and aesthetic requirements. It is important for us to remain open and flexible to future change. In this way, we ensure that our buildings and spaces also meet the needs of users in the long term.

For the sporting goods retailer Bründl in the Austrian Alps, for example, we built the flagship store in Kaprun in 2008 and expanded it in 2021. From the very first brushstroke our commitment was decisive at every level. We continued our building, which was awarded the Austrian State Prize, in a respectful yet innovative way: We wanted to make it even more sustainable. Our efforts paid off. The Austrian Sustainable Building Council (ÖGNI) awarded us the platinum seal for interior design and restaurant. It is the first such award for interiors in Austria. A success that is equally attributable to the aims of our client, our expertise and the synergies achieved. For Bründl, we not only took on the structural and interior work, but also designed the navigation and communication.

Konservatives Ziel, progressives Handeln

Mit diesem Geist wollen wir die nächsten Jahre nutzen, um klimaneutral zu werden. Hierfür müssen wir nicht nur das Bauen neu denken, sondern auch die Stadt, die Kommunikation, das Design. Der gesellschaftliche und wirtschaftliche Wandel hat sich in den letzten Jahrzehnten atemberaubend beschleunigt und wir müssen uns darauf einstellen, dass die Geschwindigkeit in nächster Zeit nicht nachlassen wird. In diesem Kontext auf Nachhaltigkeit und Langlebigkeit zu setzen, heißt also auch: Haltung zeigen. Ein ikonischer Satz aus Giuseppe Tomasi di Lampedusas Roman *Der Leopard*, in dem es um das Leben einer sizilianischen Adelsfamilie zur Zeit der großen politischen, gesellschaftlichen und wirtschaftlichen Umbrüche im späten 19. Jahrhundert geht, kann auch als Maxime für unsere Zeit gelten: „Wenn wir wollen, dass alles so bleibt, wie es ist, muss alles sich ändern." Nur durch Fortschritt können wir unseren Planeten retten – progressives Handeln für ein konservatives Ziel.

Gestaltung heißt für blocher partners – gegründet 1989 von Jutta und Dieter Blocher – ganzheitliche, nachhaltige Erlebniskonzepte zu kreieren. Die Grundlage bilden die Werte Kreativität und Innovation, Kundenfokus, Verbindlichkeit und Verantwortung, Lernen, Transdisziplinarität und das Miteinander. Über 250 Architekten, Innenarchitekten, Produktdesigner und Kommunikationsexperten entwickeln so in Stuttgart, Berlin, Mannheim und Ahmedabad Bauvorhaben für die öffentliche Hand wie auch private Wohnhäuser, Hotels, Bürogebäude, Stores und Hybridbauten. Seit einigen Jahren ergänzen die Kommunikationsagentur typenraum, blocher partners General Planning sowie blocher partners sens die Unternehmensgruppe. Mit der Gründung von blocher partners sustain bietet die Unternehmensgruppe seit 2023 auch Beratung rund um das Thema nachhaltiges Planen und Bauen an.
www.blocherpartners.com

Conservative goal, progressive action

It is in this spirit that we want to use the next few years to become carbon neutral. To achieve this, we not only have to rethink building, but also the city, communication and design. Social and economic change has accelerated at a breathtaking speed in recent decades and shows no signs of slowing down any time soon. Focusing on sustainability and longevity in this context therefore also involves taking a stance. An iconic line from Giuseppe Tomasi di Lampedusa's novel The Leopard, which is about the life of a Sicilian aristocratic family at a time of great political, social and economic upheaval in the late 19th century, can also serve as a maxim for our times: "If we want things to stay as they are, things will have to change." Only through progress can we save our planet – progressive action for a conservative goal.

For blocher partners – founded in 1989 by Jutta and Dieter Blocher – design means creating holistic, sustainable experience concepts. The basis for their work are the values creativity and innovation, customer focus, commitment and responsibility, learning, transdisciplinarity and cooperation. More than 250 architects, interior designers, product designers and communication experts in Stuttgart, Berlin, Mannheim and Ahmedabad develop construction projects for the public sector as well as private homes, hotels, office buildings, shops and hybrid buildings. For several years now, the group has been complemented by the communication agency typenraum, blocher partners General Planning and blocher partners sens. With the founding of blocher partners sustain, the group has also been offering advice on sustainable planning and construction since 2023.
www.blocherpartners.com

CULTIVATING THE FUTURE OF RETAIL WITH EDUCATION AND INNOVATION

GABI STUMVOLL & DR. MAXIMILIAN PEREZ, RID STIFTUNG

Die Günther Rid Stiftung für den bayerischen Einzelhandel ist aus dem unternehmerischen Erfolg des Münchner Traditionshauses BETTENRID, heute ein stiftungseigenes und managementgeführtes Multi-Channel-Fachgeschäft, hervorgegangen. Mit der Stiftungsgründung 1988 legte Dr. Günther Rid den Grundstein dafür, die Existenz eines starken und innovationsfreudigen mittelständischen Einzelhandels zu sichern und damit auch einen Beitrag zum Erhalt einer vielfältigen Stadtkultur zu leisten. Die Stiftung fördert seit mehr als 35 Jahren Händler:innen aus ganz Bayern mit hochkarätigen, für die Teilnehmenden kostenfreien Fortbildungsprogrammen.

Der Einzelhandel ist die drittgrößte Wirtschaftsbranche in Deutschland und essenziell für die Nahversorgung und Attraktivität der Städte. Angesichts der Digitalisierung steht er vor großen Herausforderungen. Die Rid Stiftung unterstützt mit kostenlosen Weiterbildungen, die ganz gezielt auf die Bedürfnisse des mittelständischen Einzelhandels ausgerichtet sind.

The Günther Rid Stiftung für den bayerischen Einzelhandel grew out of the entrepreneurial success of the heritage Munich-based company BETTENRID, today a foundation-owned multi-channel specialist retailer. With the establishment of the Foundation in 1988, Dr. Günther Rid created the basis for securing the existence of a strong and innovative small and medium-sized retail sector, thus also contributing to the preservation of a diverse urban culture. For more than 35 years, the Foundation has been supporting retailers throughout Bavaria with top-class training programmes that are free of charge to participants.

The retail sector is the third largest economic sector in Germany and is essential for the local supply of the community and attractiveness of towns and cities. With digitalisation advancing, it faces huge challenges. The Rid Foundation provides support in the form of free further training courses that are tailored to the specific needs of small and medium-sized retailers.

Im Herzen Münchens: der Sitz der Rid Stiftung und der BETTENRID Flagship Store in der Theatinerstraße.
At the heart of Munich: the Rid Foundation headquarters and the BETTENRID flagship store in the Theatinerstrasse.

Das Team der Rid Stiftung (v. l. n. r.): Dr. Maximilian Perez (Innovationsförderung), Michaela Pichlbauer (Vorständin), Dagmar Harnest (Leitung Stiftungsbüro), Maria Fischer (Finanzen und Organisation), Gabi Stumvoll (Kommunikation und Marketing).
The Rid Foundation team (from left to right): Dr. Maximilian Perez (Innovation Management), Michaela Pichlbauer (Chairwoman), Dagmar Harnest (Foundation Office Manager), Maria Fischer (Finances and Organisation), Gabi Stumvoll (Communication and Marketing).

Über 1.000 Einzelhändler und Einzelhändlerinnen nehmen jedes Jahr an den kostenfreien Förderangeboten in den Bereichen Führung, Persönlichkeitsentwicklung, Marketing, Unternehmensnachfolge und E-Commerce teil. Neben mehrtägigen Seminaren werden auch einjährige Coachingprogramme für Unternehmen angeboten. Ein zertifizierter Abschluss als Datenexpert:in oder E-Commerce Manager:in ist ebenfalls möglich. Das Herzstück der Stiftung ist ein fünfwöchiges, praxisorientiertes Qualifizierungsprogramm für Unternehmer:innen – eine Art praxisorientiertes „Best of"-BWL-Studium. Neben den fachlichen Herausforderungen steht auch immer die Persönlichkeitsentwicklung der Unternehmer:innen im Mittelpunkt.

Die Förderangebote werden von der Rid Stiftung zusammen mit ihren Netzwerkpartnern stetig weiterentwickelt und ausgebaut. Aktuelle Trends und Themen, wie beispielsweise der Einsatz von künstlicher Intelligenz oder Nachhaltigkeit im Einzelhandel, werden berücksichtigt. Im knapp einjährigen Coachingprogramm „Digitalisierung und Nachhaltigkeit" wird vor allem auf die Aspekte Wirtschaftlichkeit und Machbarkeit in der Umsetzung eingegangen. Im Fokus der aktuellen Stiftungsarbeit stehen die Zukunftsthemen Innovation, Kooperation und Digitalisierung. In verschiedenen Förderprogrammen, Wettbewerben, Studien und Kongressen bringt die Rid Stiftung verschiedene Akteure aus dem Handel, der Politik und Wissenschaft zusammen und organisiert Branchenevents.

Every year, over 1,000 retailers attend training courses in leadership, personal development, marketing, business succession and e-commerce offered free of charge by the Foundation. In addition to seminars lasting several days, one-year coaching programmes are also offered for companies. A certified degree as a data expert or an e-commerce manager is also possible. At the heart of the Foundation is a five-week, practice-orientated qualification programme for entrepreneurs – a kind of "best of" business studies for practitioners. Besides the professional challenges, they always also focus on the personal development of the entrepreneurs.

The Rid Foundation, together with its network partners, is constantly developing and expanding its training programmes. Current trends and topics, such as the use of artificial intelligence or sustainability in retail, are taken into account. In the year-long coaching programme "Digitalisation and sustainability", the focus lies on the aspects of economic efficiency and feasibility in implementation. The Foundation's current work focuses on the future topics of innovation, cooperation and digitalisation. In various training programmes, competitions, studies and congresses, the Rid Foundation brings together various players from retail, politics and science and organises industry events.

Networking plays a crucial role in retail, as it enables entrepreneurs to exchange knowledge and develop new business ideas. This is another area the Rid Foundation addresses, offering the "Retail Tour" as a format for retailers to share their experiences directly. Innovative business models are visited on site and serve as a source of inspiration for others. The "Retail Talk" format promotes the exchange between retail, politicians and administration to jointly shape retailing in the city of the future. The Rid Foundation has been cooperating with associations, ministries and local councils for many years.

The Foundation is currently focusing on the goal of actively supporting retailers in the further development and digitalisation of their brick-and-mortar business models. The "Future Retail Store" is not a showroom or laboratory. Small and medium-sized retail companies are given the opportunity to experiment with digital technologies and new business models while minimising risk. Various digital innovations are being tested experimentally on a real shop floor with real transactions and real customers and scientifically supported by the Fraunhofer Institute for Integrated Circuits IIS.

Der Future Retail Store der Urban Gardeners in München mit Plantfinder und 3D-Druck am Point of Sale.
Munich's Urban Gardeners Future Retail Store with plant finder and 3D printing at the point of sale.

Netzwerken spielt eine entscheidende Rolle im Handel, da es Unternehmern und Unternehmerinnen ermöglicht, Wissen auszutauschen und neue Geschäftsideen zu entwickeln. Auch hier setzt die Rid Stiftung an und bietet mit der „Retail Tour" ein Format zum direkten Erfahrungsaustausch für Händlerinnen und Händler an. Innovative Geschäftsmodelle werden vor Ort besucht und können als Inspirationsquelle für andere nutzbar gemacht werden. Mit dem Format „Retail Talk" wird der Austausch des Einzelhandels mit Politik und Verwaltung zur gemeinsamen Gestaltung des Handels in der Stadt der Zukunft gefördert. Die Rid Stiftung kooperiert hierbei seit vielen Jahren mit Verbänden, Ministerien und Kommunen.

Aktuell widmet sich die Rid Stiftung verstärkt dem Ziel, Händler:innen direkt bei der Weiterentwicklung und Digitalisierung ihrer stationären Geschäftsmodelle zu unterstützen. Der „Future Retail Store" ist kein Showroom oder Labor. Mittelständische Handelsunternehmen erhalten die Möglichkeit, mit digitalen Technologien und neuen Geschäftsmodellen risikominimiert zu experimentieren. Auf einer realen Ladenfläche mit realen Transaktionen und realer Kundschaft werden experimentell verschiedene digitale Innovationen getestet und wissenschaftlich durch das Fraunhofer-Institut für Integrierte Schaltungen IIS begleitet.

Geschäftsführer der Urban Gardeners: Jakob und Valentin Kiefl.
CEOs of the Urban Gardeners: Jakob and Valentin Kiefl.

2024 öffnen im Münchner Rathaus im Rahmen des Formats Future Retail Store die Urban Gardeners eine grüne Oase und präsentieren ein Sortiment, das speziell auf die Bedürfnisse urbaner Lebensräume zugeschnitten ist. Dafür werden aktuelle Trends mittels Social-Media-Analysen erkannt und passende Produkte angeboten. Interaktive Screens und ein KI-Chatbot bieten den Kundinnen und Kunden eine innovative Einkaufserfahrung. Vor Ort werden zudem Übertöpfe mittels 3D-Druck produziert und verkauft.

Im gleichen Jahr erprobt – ebenfalls im Rahmen des Future Retail Store – auf der eigenen Ladenfläche in Nürnberg die Cairo AG eine innovative Hologramm-Beratung. Bei dieser wird Fachpersonal als holografisches Bild an den Point of Sale „teleportiert". So kann die Kundschaft an verschiedenen Standorten gleichzeitig eine persönliche Beratung erhalten. Die Erkenntnisse aus dem Projekt werden fortlaufend mit Fachleuten aus Handel, Stadtentwicklung und Wissenschaft geteilt, um die Zukunft von Stadt und Handel gemeinsam gestalten zu können.

In 2024, Urban Gardeners will open a green oasis in Munich Town Hall as part of the Future Retail Store format, presenting a product range that is specially tailored to the needs of urban living spaces. To this end, current trends are identified using social media analyses and suitable products are offered. Interactive screens and an AI chatbot let customers have an innovative shopping experience. In addition, plant pots are produced and sold on site using 3D printing.

In the same year, Cairo AG tested an innovative hologram consultation service – also as part of the Future Retail Store – on its own shop floor in Nuremberg. This involves specialist staff being "teleported" to the point of sale as a holographic image. It means that customers can receive personal advice at different locations at the same time. The findings from the project are shared on an ongoing basis with experts from retail, urban development and science to co-shape the future of cities and retail.

Die Günther Rid Stiftung für den bayerischen Einzelhandel fördert seit mehr als 35 Jahren mittelständische Händlerinnen und Händler in Bayern mit kostenfreien Aus- und Weiterbildungen sowie intensiven Coachingprogrammen. Die kostenfreien Angebote sind speziell auf die Bedürfnisse und praktischen Erfordernisse des mittelständischen Handels ausgerichtet und werden stetig weiterentwickelt. Im Fokus der aktuellen Stiftungsarbeit stehen auch die Zukunftsthemen Innovation, Kooperation und Digitalisierung. In verschiedenen Förderprogrammen, Wettbewerben, Studien und Veranstaltungen bringt die Rid Stiftung regelmäßig verschiedene Akteure aus dem Handel, der Wirtschaft, Wissenschaft und Politik zusammen.
www.rid-stiftung.de
www.futureretailstore.de

The Günther Rid Stiftung für den bayerischen Einzelhandel has been supporting small and medium-sized retailers in Bavaria for more than 35 years with free training and further education as well as intensive coaching programmes. The free services are specially tailored to the needs and practical requirements of small and medium-sized businesses and are constantly being enhanced and refined. The foundation's current work also focuses on the future topics of innovation, cooperation and digitalisation. In various training courses, competitions, studies and events, the Rid Foundation regularly brings together various players from the worlds of retail, business, science and politics.
www.rid-stiftung.de
www.futureretailstore.de

SPACES

58

92

26

108

58

38

26

30

50

116

92

42

128

76

34

BYD PIONEER STORE

LOCATION STUTTGART, GERMANY **CLIENT** HEDIN ELECTRIC MOBILITY GMBH, STUTTGART **CONCEPT / DESIGN** ATELIER BRÜCKNER, STUTTGART **LIGHTING** SCHATZ+LICHTDESIGN, STUTTGART **MEDIA** MEDIENPROJEKT P2, STUTTGART; AMPLIFY DESIGN GMBH, STUTTGART **PHOTOGRAPHS** ATELIER BRÜCKNER MICHAEL REINER, STUTTGART

Inspiriert vom Firmen-Leitsatz „Build Your Dreams", wirkt der BYD Pioneer Store in der vor Kurzem revitalisierten Calwer Passage in der Stuttgarter Innenstadt wie eine Boutique, die zum Flanieren einlädt. Die 1995 gegründete Marke spielt in den Branchen Elektronik, Automobil, erneuerbare Energien und Schienennahverkehr eine führende Rolle und ist in China bereits die größte Automarke nach Verkaufszahlen. Nun will BYD auch den europäischen Markt erobern. Für den Markteintritt in Deutschland setzt das Unternehmen unter anderem auf „Pioneer Stores" in Premiumlagen deutscher Großstädte, um Passanten und potenzielle Kunden gleichermaßen anzusprechen. ATELIER BRÜCKNER entwickelte dafür die Design-Guideline und hat diese als Erstes in Stuttgart umgesetzt.

Inspired by the company motto "Build Your Dreams", the BYD Pioneer Store in the recently revitalised Calwer Passage in Stuttgart's city centre looks like a boutique that invites visitors to browse. Founded in 1995, the brand plays a leading role in the electronics, automotive, renewable energy and local rail transport sectors and is already the largest automotive marque in China in terms of sales figures. Now BYD is looking to penetrate the European market. For its entry into the German market, the company is focusing on Pioneer Stores in premium locations in major German cities in order to appeal to passersby and potential customers alike. ATELIER BRÜCKNER developed the design guidelines for these stores and was the first to implement them in Stuttgart.

SPACES BYD PIONEER STORE

The Dreamscape design created and implemented by ATELIER BRÜCKNER combines urban architecture with interactive media stations. An interactive LED wall that reacts to movement welcomes visitors, while media elements such as the Car Configurator and the Technic Table encourage interaction with the brand. As "Pioneers", the urban stores want to make the brand and its products better known in Germany, bringing them directly to the public. The underlying design concept is modular, flexible and smart, expressing the company's three-dimensional brand language.

Das von ATELIER BRÜCKNER entworfene und umgesetzte „Dreamscape"-Design verbindet urbane Architektur mit interaktiven Medienstationen. So begrüßt eine auf Bewegung reagierende, interaktive LED-Wand die Besuchenden, während Medienelemente wie der Car Configurator und der Technic-Table zur Interaktion mit der Marke auffordern. Die urbanen Stores sollen als „Pioneers" die Marke und ihre Produkte in Deutschland bekannter machen und direkt zum Publikum bringen. Zugrunde liegt dem ein modulares, flexibles und smartes Designkonzept, das die dreidimensionale Markensprache des Unternehmens zum Ausdruck bringt.

Architektonische Elemente wie Arkaden, Treppen und Asphalt kontrastieren mit den technischen Aspekten der Marke. Grundformen wie Kugeln, Würfel und Kreissegmente bilden die Basis des Retail Designs. Die Gestaltenden haben diese Elemente in einer Design-Guideline für zukünftige Standorte in den Toplagen deutscher Innenstädte (wie Hamburg, Frankfurt, München, Köln und Berlin) zusammengefasst.

Architectural elements such as arcades, stairs and asphalt contrast with the technical aspects of the brand. Basic shapes such as spheres, cubes and discs form the basis of the retail design. The designers have compiled these elements into a design guideline for future stores in the top locations of German city centres (Hamburg, Frankfurt, Munich, Cologne, Berlin, among others).

Übrigens: Entgegen der nahe liegenden Interpretation steht das griffige Kürzel BYD nicht ursprünglich für Build Your Dreams (englisch für „Bau dir deine Träume"), sondern ist die Abkürzung des chinesischen Firmennamens BïYàDí.

By the way: Contrary to what you might think, the catchy acronym BYD does not originally stand for Build Your Dreams but is short for the Chinese company name BïYàDí.

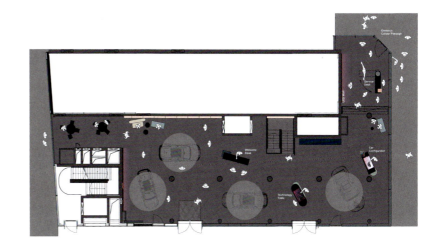

MAISON M-I-D 1985

LOCATION OSAKA, JAPAN   **CLIENT** M-I-D, OSAKA   **CONCEPT / DESIGN** CURIOSITY, TOKYO
LIGHTING MODULEX INC., TOKYO   **PHOTOGRAPHS** SATOSHI SHIGETA, TOKYO

In Umeda, dem Herzen Osakas, gelegen, verkörpert der neue Concept Store von m-i-d, Maison m-i-d 1985, den pulsierenden Geist der Fashionistas von Osaka in einer überraschenden Explosion kräftiger Farben. Umeda ist der zentrale innerstädtische Kopfbahnhof der nördlichen Eisenbahn und hochfrequentierter Bezirk für Handel, Business, Shopping und Entertainment in Kita-ku. Während der letzten Jahre wurde der ganze Distrikt umfassend überarbeitet und weitere Verbesserungen stehen an. Wie ein Leuchtturm zieht der auffällige Store auf der 4. Etage des modernen, denkmalgeschützten Hankyu Umeda Department Stores – eines der beliebtesten Kaufhäuser Osakas – die Flanierenden an.

Located in Umeda, at the heart of Osaka, m-i-d's new concept store, Maison m-i-d 1985, embodies the vibrancy and spirit of Osaka's fashion lovers, with an unexpected burst of bold colours. Umeda is the city's main northern railway terminus and a major commercial, business, shopping and entertainment district in Kita-ku. The whole district has undergone a major facelift over the past few years, and more improvements are scheduled. Like a beacon, the eye-catching store is a magnet for passers by on the 4th floor of the sophisticated heritage Hankyu Umeda Department Store, one of Osaka's most popular stores.

SPACES   MAISON M-I-D 1985

CURIOSITY, das mit der Realisation des Stores beauftragt war, ist ein in Tokio ansässiges mulitidisziplinäres Studio des französischen Designers Gwenael Nicolas. Unverkennbar sind seine Designs: transluzent, emotional und attraktiv. Das lichtdurchlässige knallgelbe Glas bestimmt als Material Ton und Design des gesamten Raums und verleiht dem Store mithilfe einheitlicher Veredlungen und Oberflächen eine unverkennbare Identität als Hybrid aus Kunstinstallation und magischem Ort, der schon von Weitem ins Auge sticht.

CURIOSITY, who was tasked with the store's realisation, is a multidisciplinary studio based in Tokyo, created by French designer Gwenael Nicolas. Its designs are unmistakable: translucent, emotional and attractive. The vibrant yellow translucent glass material sets the tone and defines the design for the entire space, creating a unique identity for the store that is unified by a series of finishes and surfaces. It is somewhere between an art installation and a magical space, drawing the eye from a distance.

Die extra entwickelten verschiedenen gelben Materialien definieren je nach Art der Produktgruppen die Bereiche, wobei die monochrome Umgebung die meist schwarzen und weißen Kleidungsstücke deutlich hervorstechen lässt. Der Raum erstreckt sich labyrinthartig, unterteilt durch große transparente gelbe Glasbausteinwände, die die vielen Ebenen optisch reflektieren und streuen. Dabei deckt sich die Leistenstruktur an der Decke exakt mit der gläsernen Fläche des Bodens, als würde sich die Umrandung in ihm spiegeln. Die durchdacht platzierte Linie ist auffällig, doch von beruhigender Wirkung. Durch die transparenten Glaswände, die zarten Töne der Bodenplatten und die Decken-Metallleisten entsteht ein rhythmischer, zugleich aber einheitlicher Raum. Die Gitterstruktur der Leisten streut das Licht und verteilt das frische Gelb im gesamten Store.

Als größter Concept Store von m-i-d bietet der Raum den Kund:innen ein beruhigendes Flair, in dem sie gemütlich das Warenangebot durchstöbern oder auf einem der extra angefertigten bequemen Sessel eine Pause einlegen können. Die Komposition von Glasbaustein-Oberflächen und abstrakten monolithischen Elementen erzeugt eine unerwartete, ikonische und eindrucksvolle Retail-Umgebung.

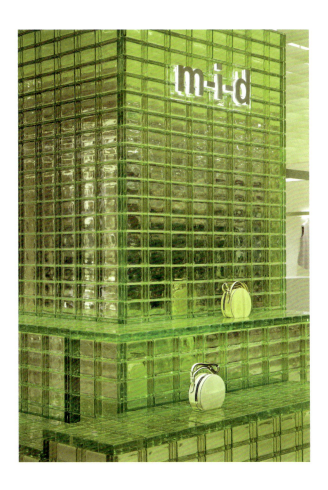

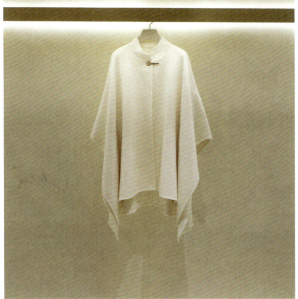

The custom-made various yellow materials define the different areas according to the characteristics of the collections. The garments, mostly in black and white, stand out in the monochrome environment. The space is laid out like a labyrinth, with large transparent partitions in yellow glass bricks that reflect and divert the layered surroundings. The louvers on the ceiling are precisely aligned with the glass laid on the floor, as if the line reflects upside down. The well-ordered line creates a striking yet comforting impression on the eye. A rhythmic yet unified space, created by the transparent glass on the walls, soft tones of the floor tiles and metal louvers on the ceiling. The latticed slats diffuse the light, bathing the entire store in a fresh shade of yellow.

As m-i-d's largest concept store, the space offers the customers a relaxing ambiance in which they browse selected items at their leisure or take a break on one of the bespoke comfortable chairs. The composition of glass brick surfaces and abstract monolithic volumes creates an unexpected, iconic and memorable retail environment.

GROHE WATER EXPERIENCE CENTER

LOCATION DUSSELDORF, GERMANY **CLIENT** GROHE AG, DUSSELDORF **CONCEPT / DESIGN** D'ART DESIGN GRUPPE, NEUSS / LIXIL GLOBAL DESIGN **PHOTOGRAPHS** SIMON WEGENER FOTOGRAFIE, BAD HONNEF

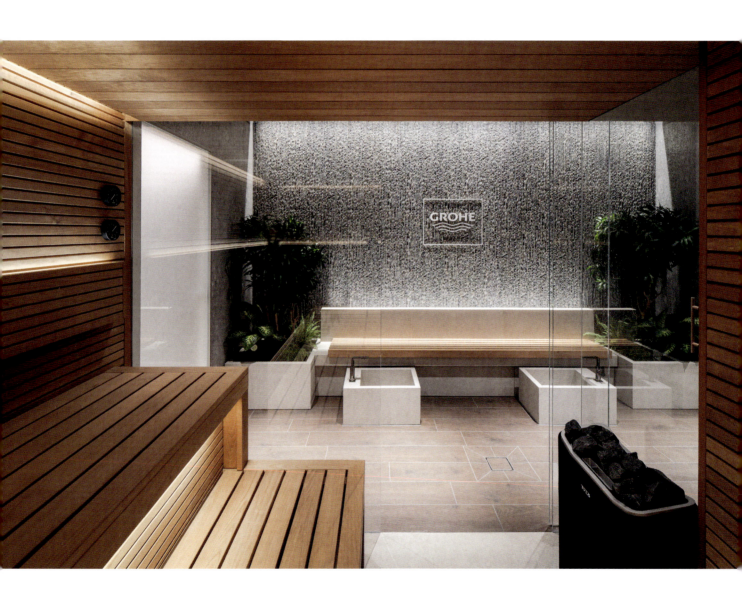

Inmitten der lebendigen Metropole Düsseldorf liegt die Repräsentanz der GROHE AG. Seit 2014 gehört das Unternehmen zum Markenportfolio der LIXIL Group, einem globalen Hersteller von Wassertechnologien und Gebäudeausstattung. Ein neues Highlight für die Kunden, das Fachpublikum und die eigenen Mitarbeiter ist das GROHE Water Experience Center. Die Produkte der exklusiven GROHE SPA Kollektion sind hier in einer authentischen Umgebung inszeniert und können live ausprobiert werden.

The representative office of GROHE AG is located in the heart of the pulsating metropolis of Dusseldorf. Since 2014, the company has been part of the brand portfolio of the LIXIL Group, a global manufacturer of water technologies and building equipment. The GROHE Water Experience Center is a new highlight for customers, trade visitors and the company's own employees. The products of the exclusive GROHE SPA collection are presented in an authentic environment and can be tried out live.

Gestaltet wurde das Experience Center von der D'art Design Gruppe, die in interdisziplinären Teams mit rund 60 kreativen Köpfen Kommunikation in jeder Dimension inszeniert: on- und offline, in Form und Inhalt, temporär und permanent. Das Konzept entstand in enger Zusammenarbeit mit dem unternehmenseigenen LIXIL Global Design und Brand Identity Team.

Der komfortable Sauna-, Spa- und Fitnessbereich hat eine geradlinige, edle Designsprache, die von ästhetischen Kontrasten geprägt ist. Warme Hölzer und kühlere Steinmaterialien, ein Wechsel von hellen und dunklen Oberflächen verbinden sich zu einer anspruchsvollen Innenarchitektur. Die hochwertige Ausstattung der großzügigen Räume und nutzerfreundliche Handhabungen stellen das Wohlbefinden in den Fokus des Erlebnisses und machen das Experience Center zu einem besonderen Ort der Produktinszenierung bei der Gestaltung von Räumen für Fitness, Wellness und Erholung.

The Experience Center was designed by D'art Design Gruppe, whose interdisciplinary teams of around 60 creative minds stage communication in every dimension: online and offline, in form and content, temporary and permanent. The concept was developed in close collaboration with the company's own LIXIL Global Design and Brand Identity Team.

The comfortable sauna, spa and fitness area has a simple, elegant design language that is characterised by aesthetic contrasts. Warm woods and cooler stone materials, an alternation of light and dark surfaces combine to create a sophisticated interior design. The high-quality furnishings of the spacious rooms and user-friendly operation put well-being at the centre of the experience and turn the Experience Center into a special place for product staging in the design of rooms for fitness, wellness and relaxation.

Das GROHE Water Experience Center ist auch als virtuelles Pendant bei GROHE X, dem digitalen Content Hub des Unternehmens, erlebbar. In der ebenfalls von der D'art Design Gruppe entwickelten Real-Time Application können die Räume und einzelnen Stationen in einem fotorealistischen virtuellen Rundgang erkundet werden. Unter dem Dach der digitalen Plattform finden die verschiedenen Zielgruppen speziell auf sie zugeschnittene Ideen und Informationen – in mehreren Sprachen. Dies ermöglicht Endverbrauchern wie auch Profis und Pressevertretern ein individuelles Markenerlebnis.

The GROHE Water Experience Center can also be experienced as a virtual counterpart at GROHE X, the company's digital content hub. The real-time application, also developed by D'art Design Gruppe, allows visitors to explore the rooms and individual stations in a photorealistic virtual tour. Under the umbrella of the digital platform, the various target groups can find ideas and information tailored specifically to them – in several languages. End consumers as well as professionals and the press can thus enjoy an individual brand experience.

SPACES GROHE WATER EXPERIENCE CENTER

ROTTLER EXKLUSIV

LOCATION ARNSBERG, GERMANY **CLIENT** BRILLEN ROTTLER GMBH & CO. KG, ARNSBERG
CONCEPT / DESIGN HEIKAUS ARCHITEKTUR GMBH, STUTTGART **LIGHTING** HEIKAUS ARCHITEKTUR GMBH, STUTTGART
PHOTOGRAPHS CHRISTOPH MEINSCHÄFER, ARNSBERG-NEHEIM

Zwei benachbarte Ladengeschäfte wurden per Durchbruch verbunden und zu einem großzügigen Raum zusammengefasst. So konnte direkt an der Ursprungsstätte im sauerländischen Arnsberg-Neheim, wo 1946 Maria und Paul Rottler sen. ihren ersten Augenoptikerbetrieb gründeten, ein großzügiger Store entstehen. Mittlerweile zählt das Unternehmen, das 2022 die 100-Filialen-Marke offiziell geknackt hat, zu den acht größten Augenoptikern in Deutschland. Nach zweijähriger Umbauphase eröffnete im März 2024 der erste Store unter dem neuen Namen ROTTLER Exklusiv.

Two neighbouring shops have been connected by a breakthrough and combined to form a spacious store on the original site in Arnsberg-Neheim in the Sauerland region, where Maria and Paul Rottler Sr. opened their first optician's shop in 1946. The company, which officially passed the 100-store mark in 2022, is now one of the eight largest opticians in Germany. After a two-year renovation phase, the first store opened in March 2024 under the new name ROTTLER Exklusiv.

Auf einer Fläche mit rund 132 Quadratmetern, die besonders durch die hohen Decken auffallen, inszenierten und realisierten die Planer:innen von Heikaus Architektur einen luftigen Raum, der viel Platz zur Präsentation der verschiedenen Marken bietet. Um die außergewöhnliche Deckenhöhe in Szene zu setzen, platzierten die Gestaltenden aus Stuttgart schlanke Stangen im Raum, an denen vertikale Spiegel befestigt sind. Auch die klassisch-modernen Kronleuchter finden hier eine entsprechende Raumhöhe, um ihre repräsentative Wirkung zu entfalten. Mit der Kombination der filigran gerahmten Spiegel und den Präsentationsvitrinen entsteht der Eindruck eines kleinen, aber feinen Spiegelkabinetts. Das Farbkonzept beinhaltet frisches Petrol, Minze, mattes Schwarz und Perlgold. Die Unternehmensfarbe Grün findet sich farblich angepasst in der Sonnenbrillenwand wieder, die zugleich als Eyecatcher fungiert. Ein weiterer wichtiger Punkt war die Integration einer zeitgemäßen Diebstahlsicherung mithilfe von Glasschiebetüren und elektronischen Schlössern der Vitrinen. So werden die hochwertigen Brillen der Präsentationswand geschützt.

On a footprint of around 132 square metres, which is particularly striking due to the high ceilings, the designers from Heikaus Architektur designed and implemented an airy space that offers plenty of room for the presentation of the various brands. To accentuate the extraordinary ceiling height, the designers from Stuttgart placed slender poles in the room, to which vertical mirrors are attached. Classic, modern chandeliers also find the right room height for their prestigious effect. The combination of the delicately framed mirrors and the display cabinets gives the impression of a small but fine mirror cabinet. The colour scheme includes fresh petrol, mint, matt black and pearl gold. The corporate colour of green is used in the sunglasses wall, which also acts as an eye-catcher. Another important point was the integration of a modern anti-theft system with sliding glass doors and electronic locks on the display cases. This protects the high-end eyewear on the presentation wall.

Das neue Retail Design schafft eine zeitgemäße und gleichzeitig wertvoll-gediegene Atmosphäre, die durch indirekt beleuchtete Vorhänge entlang der beeindruckenden 4 Meter hohen Wände betont wird. Auch der helle Echtholzboden trägt zu dem neuen Raumeindruck bei, der das Familienunternehmen am eigenen Gründungsstandort in neuer Frische repräsentiert.

The new retail design creates a contemporary yet sophisticated atmosphere, enhanced by indirectly illuminated curtains along the impressive 4-metre-high walls. The light-coloured genuine wood flooring also contributes to the new appearance of the space, which gives a fresh look to the family-owned company in its hometown.

SALON VERDE

LOCATION VIENNA, AUSTRIA **CLIENT** SALON VERDE, VIENNA **CONCEPT / DESIGN** UMDASCH THE STORE MAKERS, AMSTETTEN **LIGHTING** UMDASCH THE STORE MAKERS, AMSTETTEN **PHOTOGRAPHS** FRANZ MICHAEL MOSER, PERSENBEUG

Ganz auf die Wünsche und Bedürfnisse von Stadtmenschen geht das neue Konzept des österreichischen Gartencenters bellaflora ein. Bereits an drei Standorten in Wien holt der Salon Verde die Natur in die Innenstadt und ist damit genau auf das urbane Leben ausgerichtet. 2022 eröffnete die erste Filiale im 2. Wiener Gemeindebezirk; 2023 folgten zwei weitere Stores im 3. und 4. Bezirk.

The new concept from Austrian garden centre bellaflora caters specifically to the wishes and needs of city dwellers. Already in three locations in Vienna, Salon Verde brings nature into the city centre and is thus perfectly in tune with urban life. The first shop opened in Vienna's 2nd district in 2022, followed by two more in the 3rd and 4th districts in 2023.

In addition to a special range of plants for the home and balcony, Salon Verde customers can find green inspiration, home accessories, natural cosmetics and culinary specialities. The umdasch Store Makers accompanied Salon Verde as general contractor from the very beginning and are responsible for the entire innovative project, including the lighting concept and sustainable shopfitting.

As part of the customer journey, various feel-good and inspirational areas were created by zoning the space with labelled signs and different materials. Special attention is paid to cooperation with regional suppliers.

Neben einem speziellen Sortiment an Pflanzen für Wohnung und Balkon findet die Kundschaft im Salon Verde grüne Inspirationen, Wohnaccessoires sowie Naturkosmetik und kulinarische Spezialitäten. Die umdasch Store Makers begleiteten den Salon Verde als Generalunternehmer von Anfang an und zeichnen für das gesamte innovative Projekt mit Lichtkonzept und nachhaltigem Ladenbau verantwortlich.

Im Rahmen der Customer Journey wurden durch die Zonierung mit beschrifteten Schildern und unterschiedlichen Materialien verschiedene Wohlfühl- und Inspirationsbereiche geschaffen. Besonders wird auf die Zusammenarbeit mit regionalen Lieferanten geachtet.

Another crucial concern is the sale of sustainable products such as planters made from potato starch or plant pots made from sun-fired ceramics and recycled plastic. Customers can buy soil or fertiliser by the "scoop" and repot the plants directly in the store. In the "earthy corner", customers can fill containers with granular fertiliser using a special dispenser. Additional services such as the rental of tote bags or a cargo bike for transporting larger products through to sustainable delivery with electric vehicles add value to life in the city.

Der Verkauf von nachhaltigen Produkten wie Blumentöpfen aus Kartoffelstärke oder Übertöpfen aus sonnengebrannter Keramik und recyceltem Kunststoff ist ein besonderes Anliegen. So kann man beispielsweise Erde oder Dünger per „Schauferl" erwerben und die Pflanzen direkt im Store umtopfen. Im „Erdigen Eck" kann Granulat-Dünger mit einem speziellen Dispenser selbstständig abgefüllt werden. Zusätzliche Services wie der Verleih von Transporttaschen oder eines Lastenfahrrads zum Transport größerer Produkte bis hin zur nachhaltigen Lieferung mit Elektrofahrzeugen bieten einen Mehrwert für das Leben in der Stadt.

Nachhaltigkeit wird im Store aber nicht nur anhand der Produkte präsentiert, sondern auch in vielen Details der Bauausführung. So sorgt zum Beispiel ein sparsames LED-Lichtkonzept für einen energieeffizienten Betrieb. Regalflächen und Möbel aus Vollholz schaffen eine wohnlich-inspirierende Atmosphäre. Besonderes Augenmerk legten die Retail Designer auf Materialien mit kurzen Lieferketten sowie auf einen möglichst geringen CO_2- Fußabdruck.

And sustainability is present in the store not only through the products, but also in many details of the construction. For example, an economical LED lighting concept ensures energy-efficient operation. Shelving and solid wood furniture create a homely and inspiring atmosphere. The retail designers made sure to use materials with short supply chains and the smallest carbon footprint.

MEST MARZIPAN LÜBECK

LOCATION LÜBECK, GERMANY **CLIENT** MEST-MARZIPAN GMBH, LÜBECK
CONCEPT / DESIGN D.S.D.5 PLANUNGSGESELLSCHAFT MBH, MÜLHEIM A.D. RUHR **GRAPHICS** BÜRO SCHMIDT, SOLINGEN
LIGHTING CANDUS GMBH, LANGENFELD **OTHERS** SEIBEL UND WEYER GMBH, BOTTROP (SHOPFITTING); WOLFGANG SAUL GEBÄUDEAUSBAU GMBH, HAMBURG (INTERIOR WORK) **PHOTOGRAPHS** MAX SCHULZ, MÜLHEIM A.D. RUHR

Lübecker Marzipan ist eine von der EU geschützte geografische Herkunftsbezeichnung für Produkte aus der norddeutschen Stadt Lübeck und den angrenzenden Gemeinden. Bereits seit den 1950er-Jahren produziert die Familie Mest dort Marzipan. Was als Hobby von Lothar Mest begann und inzwischen von seiner Tochter Sabine Mest fortgeführt wird, ist über die Jahre zu einer der ersten Adressen für Lübecker Marzipan aus der Hansestadt Lübeck geworden. Die große Nachfrage nach ihren Produkten zog für die MEST-MARZIPAN GmbH die Notwendigkeit nach sich, ihren Stadtverkauf in Lübeck zu erweitern und auf eine größere Fläche umzuziehen.

Lübeck marzipan is an EU-protected geographical indication of origin for products from the northern German city of Lübeck and the neighbouring municipalities. The Mest family has been producing marzipan there since the 1950s. What began as Lothar Mest's hobby, now carried on by his daughter Sabine Mest, has over the years become one of the top addresses for Lübeck marzipan. The high demand for its products made it necessary for MEST-MARZIPAN GmbH to expand its city shop in Lübeck and move to larger premises.

Die Familie Mest hat sich entschieden, die Konzeptentwicklung sowie die komplette Umsetzung und Projektsteuerung für den neuen Store in die Hände der D.S.D.5 Planungsgesellschaft aus Mülheim an der Ruhr zu legen. Für das Innenarchitektur-Team war es eine spannende Aufgabe, eine komplett neue Außendarstellung zu entwickeln. Auch die Räumlichkeiten, die in Teilen aus dem 14. Jahrhundert stammen, hatten es in sich: „Eine Herausforderung war die historische Bausubstanz des Gebäudes, die technisch und baurechtlich auf den heutigen Stand zu bringen war."

The Mest family decided to entrust the concept development, complete implementation and project management for the new store to D.S.D.5 Planungsgesellschaft from Mülheim an der Ruhr. For the interior design team, it was an exciting task to develop a completely new external image. The rooms, some of which date back to the 14th century, were a task of their own: "One challenge was the historical fabric of the building, which had to be brought up to today's standards in terms of technology and building regulations."

Historische Elemente in Form von rauen Ziegelwänden sowie Fotos und Zitate aus der Firmengeschichte nehmen die Kundschaft mit auf eine Reise durch die Produkte und Produktionsweise. Insgesamt ist die Verkaufsfläche klar strukturiert, funktionale Regalelemente bieten Umbaumöglichkeiten für thematische und saisonale Anpassungen. Kontrastierende Materialien wie Eiche, Fliesen, Ziegeln und Metalloberflächen sorgen für Spannung. Das Farbkonzept des Geschäfts ist von den zarten, roséfarbenen Schattierungen der Mandelblüte inspiriert. Die sanften Töne schaffen eine warme und einladende Atmosphäre.

Historical elements in the form of rough brick walls as well as photos and quotes from the company's history take customers on a journey through the products and production methods. Overall, the sales area is clearly structured, with functional shelving elements that can be adapted to suit different themes and seasons. Contrasting materials such as oak, tiles, bricks and metal surfaces create interest. The store's colour concept is inspired by the delicate, rose-coloured shades of almond blossom. The soft tones create a warm and inviting atmosphere.

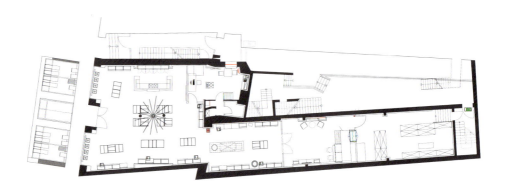

Highlight im Zentrum der Fläche ist der abstrahierte, knapp vier Meter hohe Mandelbaum, der die Hauptzutat des Marzipans symbolisiert. Nach dem Umzug und der kompletten Neugestaltung übertrifft die Kundenfrequenz im Geschäft alle Erwartungen von Familie Mest.

The highlight in the centre of the space is the abstract, almost four-metre-high almond tree that symbolises the main ingredient of marzipan. After the relocation and the complete redesign of the store, the customer frequency exceeds the Mest family's wildest expectations.

BUCHERER FINE JEWELLERY

LOCATION FRANKFURT AM MAIN, GERMANY **CLIENT** BUCHERER AG, LUZERN **CONCEPT / DESIGN** BLOCHER PARTNERS, STUTTGART **PHOTOGRAPHS** PATRICIA PARINEJAD, BERLIN; FABIAN AURÉL HILD, FRANKFURT AM MAIN

Das Uhren- und Schmuckhaus Bucherer eröffnete in Frankfurter Premiumlage seine „Bucherer Fine Jewellery Boutique". Seit 1888 gehört das Familienunternehmen zu den traditionsreichsten Häusern der Uhren- und Schmuckbranche. Eine besonders fruchtbare Partnerschaft ging Ernst Bucherer 1924 mit Hans Wilsdorf, dem Gründer der Firma Rolex, ein: Er nahm die damals noch kaum etablierte Uhrenmarke in sein Sortiment auf. Als selbstständige Marke setzt die Luzerner Firma nun ein Statement für die historischen Wurzeln des Unternehmens im Schmuckhandel.

The watch and jewellery retailer Bucherer has opened its "Bucherer Fine Jewellery Boutique" in a prime location in Frankfurt. Founded in 1888, the family business is one of the most traditional companies in the watch and jewellery industry. Ernst Bucherer entered into a particularly fruitful partnership with Hans Wilsdorf, the founder of Rolex, in 1924 when he added the then little-known watch brand to his assortment. As an independent brand, the Lucerne-based company is now making a statement about its historical roots in the jewellery trade.

Den zweigeschossigen Store in einem Bestandsgebäude auf der Goethestraße entwarfen blocher partners aus Stuttgart, mit denen Bucherer schon seit mehr als zehn Jahren zusammenarbeitet. Das Entrée wurde als gläsernes Portal gestaltet, dessen metallische Rahmung in wechselnd matten und glänzenden Schichten aufgebaut ist, was der Fassade optische Tiefe verleiht. Im Erdgeschoss dreht sich alles um die hauseigene Schmuckkollektion und Diamanten. Für die Präsentation der Produkte entwickelten die Innenarchitekten und Produktdesigner ein Regalsystem aus schlanken Stahlrohren, das durch die plastische Wandgestaltung besonders zur Geltung kommt: Die Wellen aus weich fließendem Stuccolustro öffnen sich immer wieder, um den Blick auf die Rückwand aus Muschelkalk freizugeben.

The two-storey store in an existing building on Goethestrasse was designed by blocher partners from Stuttgart, with whom Bucherer has been working for more than ten years. The entrance was designed as a glass portal with a metal frame in alternating matt and shiny layers, which lends the façade visual depth. On the first floor, everything revolves around the company's own jewellery collection and diamonds. To display the products, the interior architects and product designers developed a shelving system made of slender steel tubes, accentuated by the sculptural wall design: Again and again, waves of softly flowing stuccolustro open up to reveal the shell limestone rear wall.

Während im Erdgeschoss kühle Materialien wie Stahl, Zementestrich und Stein dominieren, steigert sich die Behaglichkeit im Obergeschoss dank eines Holzbodens und holzverkleideter Wände. Eine mit facettiertem Edelstahl verkleidete Stütze wächst vom Erdgeschoss aus durch den Deckendurchbruch nach oben. In Kombination mit einem filigranen Stahl-Mobile fungiert sie als Bindeglied der beiden Geschosse.

Gefertigt wurde das Gebilde vom in Berlin lebenden Künstler Felix Stumpf, der multidisziplinär in den Bereichen Skulptur, Grafik, Malerei, Installation und Intervention arbeitet.

While the ground floor is dominated by cool materials such as steel, cement screed and stone, the upper floor is cosier, with a wooden floor and wood-panelled walls. A column clad in faceted stainless steel grows through the ceiling opening to the upper floor. Combined with a filigree steel mobile, it acts as a link between the two floors.

The construction was crafted by Felix Stumpf, a Berlin-based artist whose multidisciplinary work encompasses sculpture, graphics, painting, installation and intervention.

SENSAI FLAGSHIP STORE SHANGHAI

LOCATION SHANGHAI, CHINA **CLIENT** SENSAI COSMETICS INC., TOKYO **CONCEPT / DESIGN** CURIOSITY, TOKYO
PHOTOGRAPHS COURTESY OF SENSAI COSMETICS INC., TOKYO

Sensai hat sich über die letzten Jahrzehnte in Europa etabliert und unterhält aktuell Filialen in über vierzig Ländern. Im Zuge der weiteren Expansion in Asien hat die japanische Luxus-Kosmetikmarke nun einen Flagship Store in Shanghai, China eröffnet. Das Markenethos beruht auf dem Sahko-Skincare-Ritual, das von einer traditionellen japanischen Teezeremonie inspiriert ist. Diese Tradition, ein Sinnbild der Gastfreundschaft, gründet auf tiefem Respekt vor der Natur, einem Gespür für ästhetische Einfachheit und der Wertschätzung von Disziplin. Zum ersten Mal können Kund:innen die Produkte vor Ort in einem komfortablen Spabereich erleben und ausprobieren.

In the last few decades, Sensai has established itself in Europe and is currently represented in over forty countries. In its drive towards further expansion in Asia, the Japanese luxury cosmetics brand has opened a flaghip store in Shanghai, China. The brand ethos is centred around the Saho skincare ritual, which takes inspiration from a traditional Japanese tea ceremony. This tradition, which epitomises hospitality, involves a deep respect for nature, a sensitivity to aesthetic simplicity and an appreciation of discipline. For the first time, customers can experience and test the use of the products on site in a comfortable spa area.

Das Design des Sensai Flagship Stores, der im Oktober 2023 eröffnet wurde, stammt aus der Feder von CURIOSITY. Die Kombination von Shoppingbereich und Spa ermöglicht der Kundschaft eine einzigartige Erfahrung. Schon von außen einsehbar, entfacht das Interior mit seinem markanten Brand Icon eine starke Wirkung und weckt die Neugier der Passanten. Hauptattraktion ist ein Kronleuchter mit fein gesponnenen Fäden, die an „Koishimaru Silk", den ikonischen Wirkstoff der Sensai-Kosmetik, erinnern. Die tief mattschwarze Wand bringt das seidene Objekt besonders zur Geltung, während eine dynamische Kurve zu den verschiedenen Abteilungen führt.

The design of the Sensai flagship store in Shanghai, which was opened in October 2023, stems from CURIOSITY. Comprising a shopping area and a spa, it offers customers an exceptional experience. The interior with a strong brand icon creates a striking impression outside the store, attracting the attention of passers by. The main feature is a chandelier with delicate strings, reminiscent of "Koishimaru Silk", the iconic ingredient of Sensai cosmetics. The deep matte black wall highlights the silky object, while a dynamic curve guides customers to the different zones.

An der Decke reflektieren sich durch Spiegel zwei schwebende Kreise, was dem Raum noch mehr Tiefe verleiht. Für die Omotenashi BAR, die einen von den vier Jahreszeiten Japans inspirierten Verpackungsservice anbietet, wurden Terrazzofliesen verlegt – ein Beitrag zur Müllreduzierung, da es sich um geupcyceltes Material handelt.

Gäste des Spas beginnen ihre Reise entlang der einladenden Gartenpassage und werden im Warteraum von warmer Gastfreundlichkeit empfangen – hier kommt die moderne Interpretation der Teezeremonie zum Tragen. Aus fünf verschiedenen Düften kann der zur jeweiligen Verfassung und Gemütslage am besten passende gewählt werden. Der immersive Korridor mit seinem verschlungenen Pfad entführt die Gäste in eine vollkommen andere Welt, fernab von der Hektik des Alltags.

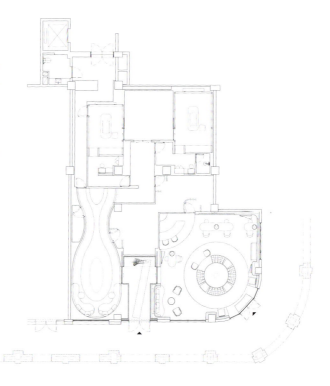

Mirror reflections create two large floating circles on the ceiling, adding generous depth to the space. The Omotenashi BAR, which offers customers special wrapping services inspired by the four seasons of Japan, is made from terrazzo tiles, an upcycled material that has been rescued from waste.

Spa guests begin their journey on the inviting garden walkway and are greeted with warm hospitality in the waiting room, which is where the modern twist on the tea ceremony comes into play. Guests can choose from five different fragrances to suit their condition and mood. The immersive corridor, with its winding path, transports visitors into a completely different world, far removed from their everyday lives.

CONCEPT STORE BY STAUDE

LOCATION HANOVER, GERMANY **CLIENT** MÖBEL STAUDE GMBH & CO. KG, HANOVER-HAINHOLZ
CONCEPT / DESIGN NOMAH INTERIOR SOLUTIONS, HANOVER **PHOTOGRAPHS** SHINO PHOTOGRAPHY, HANOVER

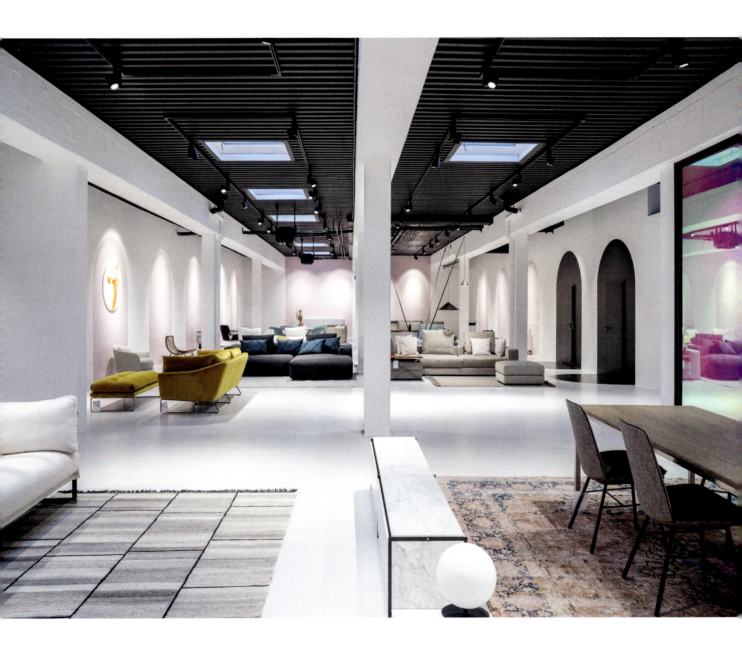

Viele Jahre war der heutige Concept Store by Staude als „SmartPrice" bekannt, der zwischen seinen „großen Brüdern", dem Möbelhaus Staude und Küchen Staude in Hannover Nord, gelegen war. Um dem Geschäft eine eigene markante Identität zu geben, hat sich der Bauherr Helmut Staude mit seinen Söhnen Alexander und Marc dazu entschlossen, ein neues Retail Design für den Laden zu entwickeln.

For many years, the current Concept Store by Staude was known as "SmartPrice", tucked away between its 'big brothers', the Staude furniture store and kitchen studio Staude in Hanover North. To give the shop its own distinctive identity, the owner Helmut Staude and his sons Alexander and Marc decided to develop a new retail design.

Friederike Müller gründete bereits neben dem Studium der klassischen Architektur und Stadtplanung ihr eigenes Büro NOMAH interior solutions, mit dem sie sich für eine nachhaltig-zeitlose, aber auch innovative wie mutige Innenarchitektur einsetzt. Das Ziel war es, einen Ort zu schaffen, an dem Kunden gerne Zeit verbringen und die Chance haben, dem Alltag zu entfliehen. „Für mich als Designerin war es wichtig, die große Verkaufsfläche so spannend und vielseitig zu gestalten, dass der Kunde wirklich alles entdecken, testen und sehen möchte und möglichst viele Produkte im Geschäft näher betrachtet werden. Dafür war eine smarte Wegeplanung durch den Grundriss wichtig und das Setzen von Fokuspunkten, um den Kund:innen die Orientierung zu erleichtern", so Friederike Müller.

Friederike Müller already founded her own architectural bureau NOMAH interior solutions while studying classical architecture and town planning, with which she commits herself to sustainable, timeless, innovative and bold interior design. Her goal was to create a place where customers would want to be and where they could escape from the hustle and bustle of everyday life. "For me as a designer, it was important to make the spacious shopfloor so exciting and versatile that the customer really wants to discover, test and see everything and take a closer look at as many products in the shop as possible. To achieve this, it was important to plan smart routes through the floor plan and create focal points to make it easier for customers to find their way around," says Friederike Müller.

Stützen und Deckenträger des Bestands wurden sichtbar belassen, die Decke teilweise mit Wellblech bekleidet und der Boden neu gegossen. Um eine gewisse „Ordnung" und Struktur zu vermitteln, gibt es Flächen, die sich durch ihre Farbgestaltung, Haptik, Textilien oder mithilfe von festen Elementen abgrenzen. Der geradlinige Grundriss ist durch organische, abgerundete Elemente aufgelockert. Dazu gehören farbige Bögen an den Wänden, die als „Kulisse" bzw. Set" für jeweils ein Designelement plus Dekoration, zum Beispiel Sessel mit Stehleuchte und Bild, dienen. Drei farbige Regalbögen neben dem Tresen / der Bar dienen dazu, kleinere Produkte zu präsentieren und zu bündeln.

Supports and ceiling beams from the existing building were left visible, the ceiling was partially clad with corrugated metal and the floor was newly poured. In order to convey a certain 'order' and structure, there are areas that are defined by colour, texture, textiles or with the help of fixed components. The linear floor plan is broken up by organic, rounded elements. These include coloured arches on the walls, which act as a set for each design element plus decoration, such as an armchair with floor lamp and picture. Three coloured shelving arches next to the counter/bar are used to display and bundle smaller products.

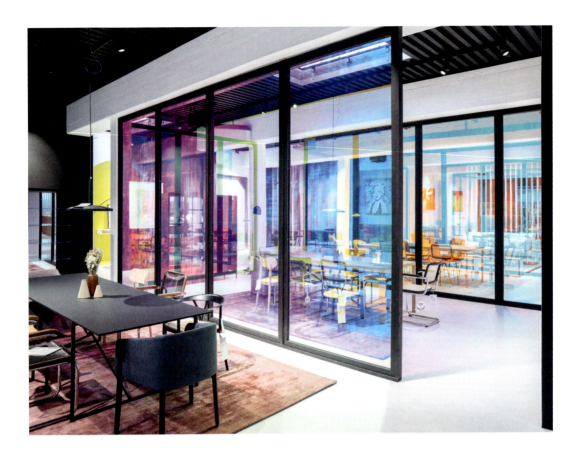

Außerdem bestand der Wunsch nach einer Küche bzw. Bar als zentralem Element, um gemeinsame Tasting-Abende und Kleinveranstaltungen ausrichten zu können. Ein spannender Bereich ist die atriumartige holografische Box. Durch die besondere Folierung der Glasscheiben in deren Innern entsteht einerseits ein Gefühl von Privatsphäre, andererseits wird der Bezug zum Rest der Umgebung gewährleistet. Je nach Blickwinkel entsteht ein neues Farbenspiel und eine andere Spiegelung. In diesem Raum im Raum können Besprechungen, Präsentationen oder auch gelegentliche Arbeitspausen stattfinden. Ein weiteres markantes Element ist die schwarze Tartanwand mit Basketballkorb, die thematisch für den Bereich Sport/Mobilität steht und besonders bei Events von der Kundschaft genutzt werden kann.

There was also a desire for a kitchen or bar as a central element to host tastings and small events. An exciting area is the atrium-like holographic box. The special foiling of the glass panes inside the box creates a sense of privacy, while at the same time creating a connection with the surroundings. Depending on the viewing angle, a new play of colours and a different reflection is created. Meetings, presentations or even occasional work breaks can take place in this room within a room. Another eyecatching element is the black tartan wall with a basketball hoop, which symbolically represents the sport and mobility theme and can be used by customers at events.

Das Konzept wurde von der Famile Staude mit Begeisterung für den mutigen und „anderen" Designansatz fast zu hundert Prozent übernommen und mit hauseigenen Tischlern und Malern umgesetzt. „Mit Sicherheit bisher das Projekt, das mir auch nachhaltig noch am meisten Freude bereitet", so die junge Architektin.

The Staude family embraced almost every element of the concept of a bold and 'different' design approach and implemented it with in-house carpenters and painters. "It is definitely the project that has given me the most lasting pleasure so far," says the young architect.

SCHÖFFEL SHOWROOM

LOCATION MUNICH, GERMANY   **CLIENT** SCHÖFFEL SPORTBEKLEIDUNG GMBH, SCHWABMÜNCHEN
CONCEPT / DESIGN KONRAD KNOBLAUCH GMBH, MARKDORF   **PHOTOGRAPHS** JENS PFISTERER, STUTTGART

Die Marke Schöffel steht für Outdoor, Ski und Sport. Und für hochwertige, nachhaltige Bekleidung, vom Spaziergang im Regen bis zum Extremabenteuer. Mit dem Claim „Ich bin raus." verdeutlicht Schöffel seinen Anspruch, exzellente Bekleidung für Menschen zu kreieren, die ihre Freizeit aktiv im Freien verbringen möchten. Als Unternehmen, das unmittelbar mit der Natur verknüpft ist, betrachtet man alle unternehmerischen Entscheidungen auch aus ökologischer und sozialer Perspektive.

The Schöffel brand is synonymous with the great outdoors, skiing and sport. And for high-quality, sustainable clothing for everything from walks in the rain through to extreme adventures. With the claim "Ich bin raus." (I'm out.), Schöffel underlines its mission to create excellent clothing for people who want to spend their leisure time actively outdoors. As a company that is directly linked to nature, all business decisions are also viewed from an ecological and social perspective.

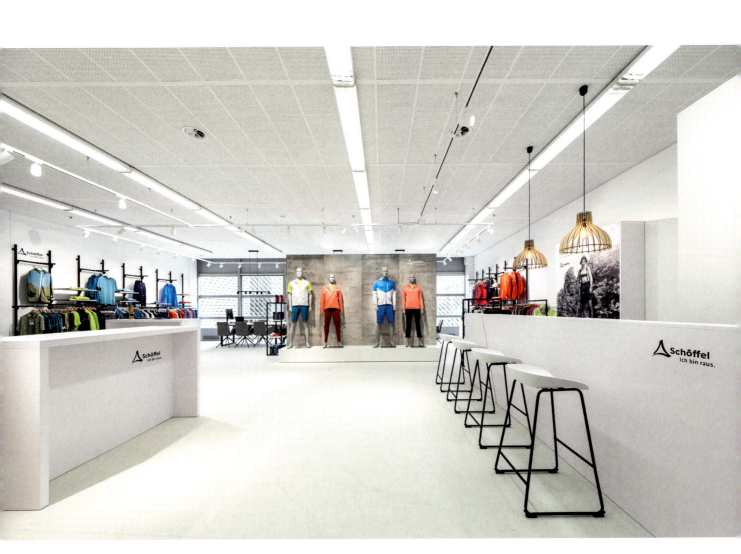

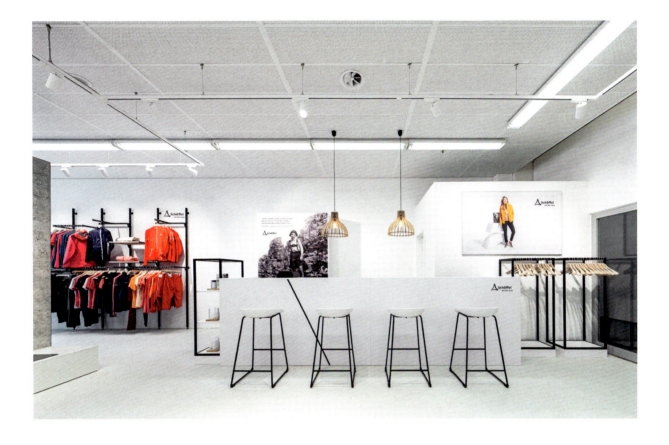

Plexiglas oder Kunststoff sucht man im neuen Showroom in München vergebens. Die Kundschaft findet dafür Holzbauteile und Fachböden aus heimischen Hölzern vor. „Auch die Betonelemente sind nicht echt. Echt? Ja, echt nicht. Es ist hauchdünner Beton auf einer Tapete. Deutsche Tapete. Der nachhaltige Trick an der Sache: Die Beton-Tapete lässt sich demontieren und wiederverwenden", so das Team der Konrad Knoblauch GmbH, die das Projekt realisiert hat.

Try as you might, you will not find plexiglas or plastic in the new showroom in Munich. Instead, customers will encounter wooden components and shelves made from local woods. "Even the concrete elements are not real. Really? Yes, they really are not real. It is wafer-thin concrete on wallpaper. German wallpaper. The sustainable trick of the matter: The concrete wallpaper can be removed and reused," says the team at Konrad Knoblauch GmbH, which realised the project.

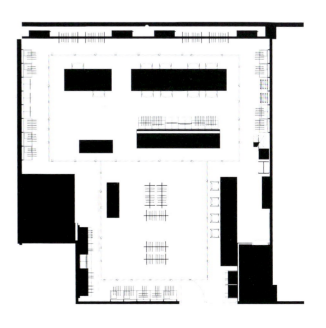

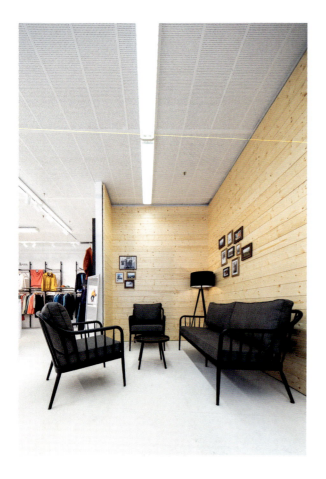

Das Erscheinungsbild der Marke ist sportiv, frisch, hell, wohnlich. Dennoch hat jeder Store seinen ganz eigenen Charakter. Den Münchener Showroom prägt die Wiederverwendung von Messemöbeln. Dazu kommen Unikate, die in der Knoblauch Manufaktur in Markdorf angefertigt wurden. Eine Herausforderung war es dabei, das Zusammenspiel zwischen neuen Möbeln und bestehenden Bauteilen abzustimmen. Es musste Platz für Hänge- und Legeware, Arbeits- und Besprechungstische sowie für einen festen Arbeitsplatz geschaffen werden. Entstanden ist ein Retail Design, das Vorfreude auf das Rausgehen macht. Oder eben, in den Worten von Schöffel: Ich bin raus.

The brand is sporty, fresh, bright and homely. Yet each store has its very own character. The Munich showroom is characterised by the reuse of trade fair furniture. There are also unique pieces made in the Knoblauch Manufaktur in Markdorf. One of the challenges here was to combine new furniture and existing substance. Space had to be created for hanging and laid goods, work and meeting tables and a fixed workstation. The result is a retail design that makes you look forward to going outdoors. Or, in the words of Schöffel: I'm out.

„Die Frage, ob nachhaltiges Store Design oder nicht, hat sich bei diesem Projekt erübrigt", erklärt das Team der Konrad Knoblauch GmbH. Mit den identity days Vol. 01 hat das Unternehmen eine Plattform für Nachhaltigkeit im Raumdesign und Innenausbau geschaffen, die im April 2024 startete. Anja Gillies und Maria Groß, Bereichsleiterinnen des interdisziplinären Raumdesigns bei Konrad Knoblauch, sind überzeugt, dass sich der Begriff Reuse in Zukunft nicht nur auf Bauteile und Materialien beschränkt, sondern in erster Linie auch den Anspruch auf Wiederverwendbarkeit in der Nutzung von Gebäuden und in der Raumgestaltung beinhaltet.

"The question of whether or not to use sustainable store design was superfluous with this project," explains the team at Konrad Knoblauch GmbH. With identity days Vol. 01, the company has created a platform for sustainability in interior design and fit-out, which was launched in April 2024. Anja Gillies and Maria Groß, heads of the interdisciplinary interior design department at Konrad Knoblauch, are convinced that the term reuse will not be limited to components and materials in future, but will also primarily include the call for reusability in the use of buildings and interior design.

ELBE RAEDEREI

LOCATION AGATHENBURG, GERMANY **CLIENT** ELBE RAEDEREI, AGATHENBURG **CONCEPT / DESIGN** THEODOR SCHEMBERG EINRICHTUNGEN GMBH, METTINGEN **PHOTOGRAPHS** REINHARD ROSENDAHL FOTOGRAFIE, VAREL

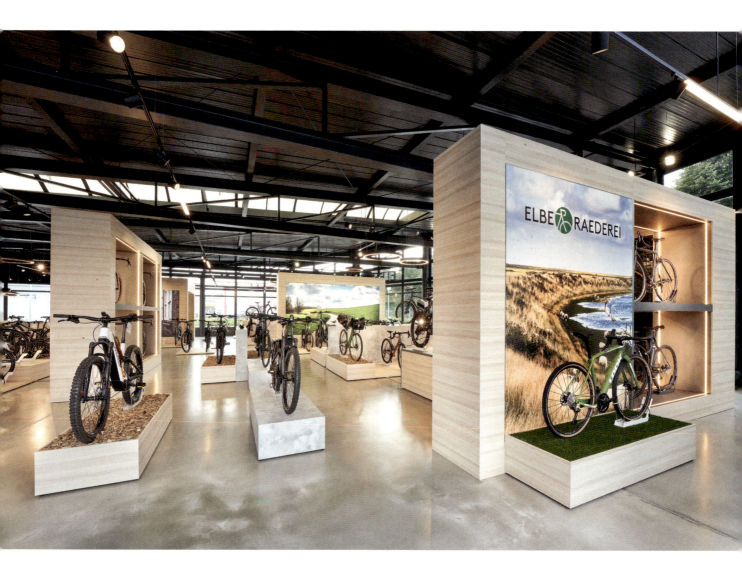

Wie in einer Werft, in der Schiffe geplant, gebaut und vom Stapel gelassen werden, können Radsportbegeisterte in der Elbe Raederei ihr Wunschfahrrad individuell konfigurieren lassen. Der Umbau des ehemaligen Autohauses des Familienunternehmens Bösch zum erlebnisorientierten Bike-Store setzt ein Zeichen für den Mobilitätswandel. Gleichzeitig weist die Raederei in Agathenburg, unweit der niedersächsischen Hansestadt Stade, auf die reizvolle Landschaft der Elbregion hin.

Just like in a shipyard where ships are designed, built and launched, cycling enthusiasts can have their dream bike individually configured at the Elbe Raederei. The conversion of the former car dealership of the Bösch family business into an experience-orientated bike shop is an example of the changing face of mobility. At the same time, the bike shop in Agathenburg, not far from the Hanseatic city of Stade in Lower Saxony, contains lots of references to the charming landscape of the Elbe region.

SPACES   ELBE RAEDEREI

Um den Wandel sichtbar zu machen, haben die Ladenbauspezialisten von Schemberg den bestehenden Auto-Showroom neu strukturiert und gestaltet. Dabei wurde die vorhandene Bausubstanz so weit wie möglich erhalten. So wurde unter anderem der rohe, industrielle Charakter der vorhandenen Kassettendecke durch einen schwarzen Anstrich betont. Im Kontrast dazu sind die Präsentationsmöbel, Wände und Böden in hellen, freundlichen Farben gehalten.

To make the change visible, the shopfitting specialists from Schemberg restructured and redesigned the existing car showroom. The original fabric of the building was preserved as far as possible. The raw, industrial character of the existing coffered ceiling, for instance, was emphasised by painting it black. This contrasts sharply with the presentation furniture, walls and floors, all in bright, friendly colours.

Im Innenraum wird die Kundschaft mit Motivwänden und Bildern aus der Region auf zukünftige Radtouren entlang der Elbe eingestimmt. Blaue Fliesen, in denen sich das Licht spiegelt und die einen Eindruck von fließendem Wasser vermitteln, schaffen eine themenbezogene Atmosphäre. Geschäftsführer Jan-Eric Bösch zur erfolgreichen Umwandlung der Räume: „Entstanden ist das Geschäft aus einem ehemaligen Autohaus. Und dessen Räumlichkeiten haben wir versucht, so weit wie möglich zu erhalten und mit natürlichen Materialien zu ergänzen. Dazu wollen wir durch verschiedene Ansätze wie etwa die Verwendung von größtenteils kaltem Wasser Energie sparen. Und auch ein umfangreiches Recyclingkonzept gehört selbstverständlich dazu."

Inside, motif walls and pictures from the region get customers in the mood for future cycling tours along the River Elbe. Blue tiles, which reflect the light and give the impression of flowing water, create a themed atmosphere. General manager Jan-Eric Bösch on the successful conversion of the premises: "The shop was originally a car dealership. We have tried to preserve the business premises as far as possible and use natural materials. We also want to save energy in various ways, mostly using cold water. Not to mention a comprehensive recycling concept."

Um den Abholprozess des neu erworbenen Bikes besonders hervorzuheben, hat Schemberg den „IHR Bike-Bereich" kreiert. Dort wird das Fahrrad für die Kundschaft, die vom Betreten des Ladens bis zum Kaufabschluss betreut und emotional abgeholt wird, gezielt in Szene gesetzt.

Schemberg has created the "YOUR bike area" to highlight the collection process of the newly purchased bike. Here, the bicycle is staged specifically for each customer, who is attended to and emotionally engaged from the moment they enter the store until they complete their purchase.

MARKTKAUF CENTER WISMAR

LOCATION WISMAR, GERMANY **CLIENT** EDEKA HANDELSGESELLSCHAFT NORD MBH, NEUMÜNSTER
CONCEPT / DESIGN KINZEL ARCHITECTURE, SCHERMBECK **GRAPHICS** KINZEL ARCHITECTURE, SCHERMBECK
PHOTOGRAPHS MIRKO KRENZEL, HANOVER

Ein neues Einkaufserlebnis mit Urlaubsatmosphäre empfängt die Kundschaft im umgebauten und von Grund auf modernisierten Marktkauf Wismar an der deutschen Ostseeküste in Mecklenburg-Vorpommern. Bereits seit Mai 1993 versorgt der Supermarkt die Kunden der Hansestadt und wurde nun unter der Leitung des Kaufmanns Karsten Heuer der Edeka Nord zum privatisierten Marktkauf mit einer Verkaufsfläche von rund 6.500 Quadratmetern.

A new shopping experience with a holiday atmosphere welcomes customers to the renovated and completely modernised Marktkauf Wismar on the German Baltic coast in Mecklenburg-Western Pomerania. The supermarket, which has been serving customers in the Hanseatic city since May 1993, was privatised from Edeka Nord and now operates as Marktkauf under the management of Karsten Heuer, with a sales area of around 6,500 square metres.

Der bestehende Markt wurde von Kinzel Architecture im laufenden Betrieb umfangreich umgebaut und revitalisiert. Dabei wurde besonders darauf geachtet, den Markt möglichst nachhaltig und energieeffizient aufzustellen. Neue verglaste Kühlmöbel, moderne Kälteanlagen, LED-Beleuchtung und Photovoltaik sorgen für eine optimierte Energieeffizienz. Neben der Technik musste auch die Gestaltung des Marktes grundsätzlich überarbeitet werden. Grundgedanke des Retail Designs ist es, das historische Stadtbild mit Küstenflair und vielfältiger Architektur im Markt erlebbar zu machen. Dafür dient als Leitmotiv ein Spaziergang entlang der Küste und über den lebendigen Marktplatz der Altstadt, die seit 2002 zum Welterbe der UNESCO gehört. Das Konzept lebt von der regionaltypischen Materialkombination aus Holz, Ziegeln, Metall, Gittern und farbigen Akzenten.

The existing store was extensively renovated and revitalised by Kinzel Architecture while it remained open for business. Special attention was paid to making the supermarket as sustainable and energy efficient as possible. New glazed refrigeration units, modern refrigeration systems, LED lighting and photovoltaics ensure optimum energy efficiency. But it is not only the technology that has been updated. The whole design of the market also had to be reworked. The basic idea behind the retail design is to bring the historic cityscape with its coastal flair and diverse architecture to life in the store. The leitmotif is a walk along the coast and through the lively market square of the old town, which was declared a UNESCO World Heritage Site in 2002. The concept has been brought to life with a combination of typical regional materials such as wood, bricks, metal, grids and colourful accents.

Eine Bodenfliese in Betonoptik zieht sich über die gesamte Verkaufsfläche, während ein „Holzsteg" aus Planken den Kundenlauf markiert und Orientierung schafft. Durch partiell aufgeklappte Holzlamellen an den Wänden werden Strandkörbe nachempfunden, die von Grünpflanzen umgeben eine naturbezogene Atmosphäre in der Obst-und-Gemüse-Abteilung verbreiten. Rings um die Verkaufsfläche sind die Küste Wismars durch eine Schichtung von schwarz-weißen Strandfotografien der Dünen, Schilfgrafiken und verspielte Holzverstrebungen spürbar. Mittig des Marktes wird durch halbtransparente Raumtrenner aus mattschwarzen Metallprofilen und farbige Akzente aus Plexiglas eine klarere Struktur für die Sortimentsbereiche geschaffen.

Marktcharakter bringen auch die Präsentationsinseln mit der darauf folgenden 20 Meter langen Frischetheke ins Spiel: Hier flanieren Kund:innen entlang der abstrahierten Skyline Wismars, die sich entlang der Deckenblenden erstreckt.

Concrete-look floor tiles run throughout the entire sales area, while a 'wooden walkway' made of planks marks the customer route and provides orientation. Partially opened wooden slats on the walls give the impression of the typical North German roofed wicker beach chairs surrounded by green plants, creating a natural atmosphere in the fruit and vegetable department. Around the sales area, black and white beach photographs of the dunes, reed graphics and quirky wooden slats have been layered to create a sense of the Wismar coast. In the middle of the store, semi-transparent room dividers made of matt black metal profiles and coloured Plexiglas accents create a clearer structure for the product ranges.

The presentation islands with the adjacent 20-metre-long fresh produce counter add a market feel of their own: Here, customers stroll along the abstract skyline of Wismar, which extends along the ceiling panels.

SC FREIBURG

LOCATION FREIBURG, GERMANY **CLIENT** SPORT-CLUB FREIBURG E.V., FREIBURG
CONCEPT / DESIGN CBA CLEMENS BACHMANN ARCHITEKTEN, MUNICH **PHOTOGRAPHS** BERND DUCKE, OTTOBRUNN

Mit über 60.000 Mitgliedern zählt der 1904 gegründete SC Freiburg zu den größten Vereinen Baden-Württembergs. Um sich langfristig wettbewerbsfähig aufzustellen und sich auch weiterhin in der Bundesliga zu etablieren, hat der SC Freiburg bereits vor Jahren entschieden, ein neues Stadion zu bauen. Dabei war es von Anfang an ein großes Anliegen, die besondere Atmosphäre des alten Dreisamstadions an der Schwarzwaldstraße in das neue zu transportieren. Einen Baustein der Begegnungskultur bilden die von CBA geplanten Besucherbereiche im Neubau, der seit Ende August 2021 Europa-Park Stadion heißt.

Founded in 1904, SC Freiburg is one of the largest clubs in Baden-Württemberg with over 60,000 members. SC Freiburg decided years ago to build a new stadium in order to remain competitive in the long term and further establish itself in the Bundesliga. From the outset, the club was keen to retain the special atmosphere of the old Dreisam Stadium on Schwarzwaldstrasse in the new one. The visitor areas designed by CBA for the new build, which has been called Europa-Park Stadium since the end of August 2021, are an integral part of the meeting culture.

So sind als Projekt der Zusammenarbeit von CBA Clemens Bachmann Architekten mit dem SC Freiburg die über drei Geschosse reichenden Hospitalityflächen des Neubaus entstanden. Die erste der drei Ebenen wurde als hochflexible Fläche gestaltet, auf der alle Arten von Events und Veranstaltungen stattfinden können. Der Raum ist frei gehalten von festen Einbauten, lediglich mobile Raumtrenner zonieren die unterschiedlichen Bereiche. An den jeweiligen Raumenden wurden Themenlounges platziert.

The three-storey hospitality areas of the new building are the result of the collaboration between CBA Clemens Bachmann Architekten and SC Freiburg. The first of the three levels has been designed as a highly flexible space for all kinds of events and functions. The space has been kept free of fixed installations, with only mobile partitions zoning the different areas. Themed lounges are located at each end of the room.

Auf der mittleren Ebene mischen sich unterschiedliche Sitz- und Aufenthaltsbereiche. So wurde in Anlehnung an das alte Schwarzwaldstadion beispielsweise die Schwarzwaldecke eingerichtet. In der SC Freiburg Club Lounge wird dagegen die sportliche Geschichte des Clubs erzählt. Über zwei große Galerieöffnungen besteht Blickbezug zum darunterliegenden Geschoss. Die mittig gelegene Bar bildet den Treffpunkt vor und nach dem Spiel. Die auf der dritten Ebene liegende Premium Lounge ist der exklusivste Teil. Hier liegt der deutlich kleinere Sitzbereich im Zentrum zwischen den Logen. Große, runde Galatische und der Teppichboden vermitteln ein elegantes, zurückhaltendes Ambiente.

The middle level is a mix of seating and lounge areas. For example, the Black Forest corner was created in the style of the old Black Forest stadium. The SC Freiburg Club Lounge, on the other hand, tells the club's sporting history. Two large gallery openings provide a view of the floor below. The centrally located bar is the meeting point before and after the match. The Premium Lounge on the third level is the most exclusive part. The much smaller seating area is located in the centre between the boxes. Large, round gala tables and the carpeting contribute to an elegant, understated ambience.

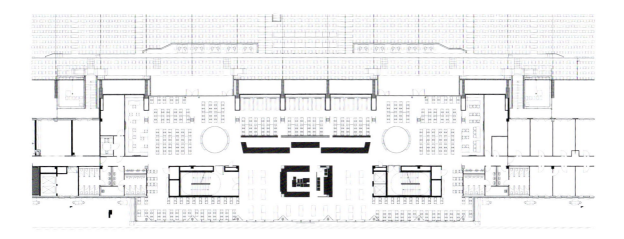

Die markanten polygonalen Linien, die sich in Form von Thekenverkleidungen, schrägen Sitzbanklehnen oder Raumteilern durch das ganze Stadion ziehen, sind konzeptionell von den Winkeln der umgebenden V-Stützen der Fassade abgeleitet. In der Premium Lounge finden sich diese als geometrisches Muster auf Wand- und Thekenverkleidungen wieder. In den Funktionsräumen im Untergeschoss wurden die Vereinsfarben Rot und Schwarz als Hauptgestaltungsmerkmal eingesetzt. Der Kontrast der beiden Farben, der über Oberflächen und Materialien transportiert wird, soll die Räume emotional aufladen und einen hohen Wiedererkennungswert schaffen.

The striking polygonal lines, which run through the entire stadium in the form of counter cladding, sloping bench backrests or room dividers, are conceptually derived from the angles of the surrounding V-columns of the façade. In the Premium Lounge, these can be found as a geometric pattern on the wall and counter panelling. The club colours red and black have been used as the main design feature in the functional rooms in the basement. The contrast of the two colours, which is conveyed by surfaces and materials, is intended to emotionally charge the spaces and create a high recognition value.

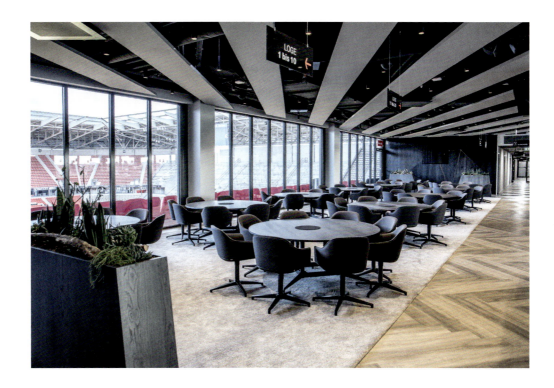

ONVIO

LOCATION NEUENKIRCHEN, GERMANY   **CLIENT** ONVIO SANITÄTSHAUS GMBH, NEUENKIRCHEN
CONCEPT / DESIGN THEODOR SCHEMBERG EINRICHTUNGEN GMBH, METTINGEN   **PHOTOGRAPHS** REINHARD ROSENDAHL FOTOGRAFIE, VAREL

Weg vom reinen Bedarfskauf hin zur ganzheitlichen kompetenten gesundheitlichen Versorgung geht es im Sanitätshaus ONVIO. Das Erscheinungsbild eines typischen Sanitätsfachgeschäfts sollte ordentlich „abgestaubt" werden. „Nach fast 30 Jahren als wachsender Gesundheitsdienstleister haben wir uns entschieden, einen Transformationsprozess einzuleiten", so die Inhaber. Ziel ist es, Menschen die ganzheitliche gesundheitliche Versorgung zu bieten, die sie benötigen, um selbstbestimmt und so lange wie möglich in den eigenen vier Wänden leben zu können.

The ONVIO medical supply store is moving away from being a shop where you buy what you need to becoming a holistic, competent healthcare provider. The image of a typical medical supply store needed to be "dusted off". "After almost 30 years as a growing healthcare provider, we have decided to start a transformation process," say the owners. The aim is to provide people with the holistic healthcare they need to live independently in their own homes for as long as possible.

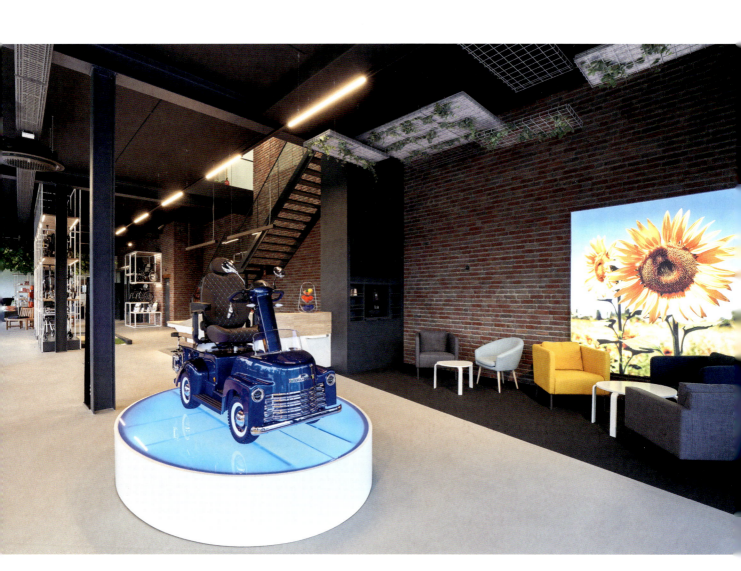

Insgesamt verfügt der Neubau in Neuenkirchen bei Rheine über eine Fläche von 1.400 Quadratmetern; allein die Ausstellungsfläche umfasst 370 Quadratmeter und ist damit die größte im Kreis und weit über die Region hinaus. Neben der großzügigen Ausstellung im Erdgeschoss beherbergt das neue Gebäude Verwaltungs-, Schulungs- und zwei Konferenzräume sowie Lagerflächen. Realisiert wurde die Neuausrichtung vom Ladenbauunternehmen Schemberg, das seit über 90 Jahren emotionale und funktionale Lösungen am Point of Sale realisiert. Der Materialmix und die Farben spiegeln das Image der neuen Marke wider und bringen die Corporate Identity auf die Fläche.

The new building in Neuenkirchen near Rheine has a total area of 1,400 square metres, of which the showroom alone is 370 square metres, making it the largest in the area and beyond. In addition to the spacious showroom on the first floor, the new building houses administration, training and two conference rooms as well as storage space. The redesign was implemented by the shopfitting company Schemberg, which has been creating emotional and functional solutions at the point of sale for over 90 years. The material mix and the colours reflect the image of the new brand and add a tangible dimension to the corporate identity.

Der Empfangstresen bietet mit einer Länge von 5 Metern ausreichend Platz, um auf die Bedürfnisse, Wünsche und Erwartungen der Kundschaft eingehen zu können. Themenwelten und Produktpräsentationen teilen den Raum auf und sorgen für Orientierung. Eine Besonderheit ist das „Demohaus", in dem Pflegehilfsmittel und wohnraumverbessernde Maßnahmen gezeigt werden. Die Rollatoren-Präsentation ermöglicht es den Kund:innen, ihr neues Hilfsmittel auf verschiedenen Bodenbelägen auszuprobieren. Die Büros wurden nach den Laufwegen der Mitarbeiterschaft im Tagesablauf angelegt. Das Gebäude wurde mit einer Solaranlage auf dem Dach und zwei Wasserstoff-Brennstoffzellen ausgerüstet, die beide Gebäude per Nahwärmeleitung mit Energie versorgen können. Somit wurde der CO_2-Fußabdruck bedeutend verbessert.

Five metres in length, the reception counter offers plenty of space to meet the needs, wishes and expectations of customers. Themed worlds and product presentations divide up the space and provide orientation. A special feature is the "demo house", where care aids and measures to improve living conditions are on display. The rollator presentation allows customers to try out their new walking aid on different floor coverings. The offices have been designed according to the employees' daily routes. The building is equipped with solar panels on the roof and two hydrogen fuel cells that can supply both buildings with energy via local heating pipes, significantly improving the carbon footprint.

Der Bereich der Mobilität ist eine Produktspezialisierung des Komplettdienstleisters im Gesundheitssektor. Deshalb wurde direkt im Eingangsbereich ein ovales Highlightpodest mit einer Präsentationsfläche für Elektromobile positioniert. Im Außenbereich wird zum Sommer hin eine Teststrecke angelegt, auf der die Kundinnen und Kunden die E-Scooter ausgiebig testen und damit auch ein Fahrsicherheitstraining absolvieren können.

Mobility is a product specialisation of the full-service healthcare provider. To emphasise this, an oval highlight platform with a presentation area for electric vehicles was positioned directly in the entrance area. During the summer months customers can test the e-scooters on a test track outdoors and take part in a driving safety training course.

DIE MUSTANG GRUPPE BRAND BOX

LOCATION TRAVELLING / POPUP EVENTS / TRADE FAIRS **CLIENT** MUSTANG STORE GMBH, SCHWÄBISCH HALL
CONCEPT / DESIGN KONRAD KNOBLAUCH GMBH, MARKDORF
PHOTOGRAPHS MUSTANG STORE GMBH, SCHWÄBISCH HALL

„Gestaltet uns einen Pop-up-Brandbooth, der zwischen verschiedenen Veranstaltungen und Festivals hin und her reist und zwischendurch unsere Marke im Headquarter inszeniert." So das Briefing von Mustang und zugleich die Geburtsstunde der Mustang Gruppe Brand Box.

"Design us a pop-up brand stand that travels back and forth between different events and festivals that can also showcase our brand at the headquarters between events." This was Mustang's brief and also the birth of the Mustang Group Brand Box.

SPACES   DIE MUSTANG GRUPPE BRAND BOX

The Mustang brand name was registered and internationally patented in 1958 as a reference to the American way of life that was so popular at the time. Back in 2019, the Schwäbisch Hall-based company set up a Corporate Responsibility Board, which defines the sustainability strategy and is responsible for its implementation. With its 360-degree marketing mix, the company focuses on the channels that are relevant for the brand and target group. Digital out-of-home ensures that the brand is also visible on the road.

The design team at Konrad Knoblauch GmbH from Markdorf on Lake Constance worked with the carpenters from the company's own factory to develop a suitable mobile shop out of a box, which when unfolded becomes a 20 square-metre pop-up store. Reflecting the brand's new urban look, the Brand Box is functional, reusable and it can be used anywhere. For events, trade fairs and festivals, indoors and outdoors as well as B2B and B2C. "It's really an XXL magic box on wheels. Filled with lots of DNA-rich design," explain the designers.

Der Markenname Mustang wurde 1958 in Anlehnung an den damals so beliebten „American Way of Life" eingetragen und international patentiert. Bereits 2019 hat das Unternehmen mit Sitz in Schwäbisch Hall ein CR-Board (Corporate Responsibility Board) ins Leben gerufen, das die Nachhaltigkeitsstrategie definiert und ihre Umsetzung verantwortet. Dabei setzt das Unternehmen mit dem 360-Grad-Marketingmix auf die Kanäle, die relevant für Marke und Zielgruppe sind. Digital out-of-home sorgt dafür, dass die Marke auch „on the road" sichtbar ist.

Das Designteam der Konrad Knoblauch GmbH aus Markdorf am Bodensee hat gemeinsam mit den Schreinern aus der hauseigenen Manufaktur einen passenden reisefähigen Shop aus der Box entwickelt, der ausgeklappt zum 20 Quadratmeter großen Pop-up-Store wird. Die Brand Box spiegelt den neuen urbanen Look der Marke wider und ist zugleich funktionell, wiederverwendbar und universell einsetzbar. Für Events, Messen und Festivals, drinnen und draußen sowie B2B und B2C. „Eigentlich ist es eine XXL-Zauberbox auf Rollen. Gefüllt mit jeder Menge DNA-geladenem Design", so die Gestalter.

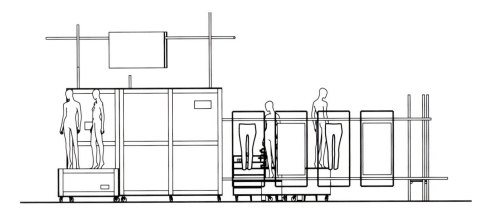

In der Brand Box finden sich: eine aufklappbare Theke, Barhocker, Kleiderstangen, Bildschirme und Präsentationsboxen. Das helle Kiefernholz und die originalen Stangen aus dem Gerüstbau verleihen dem Shop den gewünschten modern-urbanen Look. Große digitale Flächen transportieren den Spirit der Marke und auf einer Stirnwand wird auf einem Screen von 4D Magic Screen die aktuelle Kampagne präsentiert.

Das Ganze gibt es auch in kleinerem Maßstab, Pkw-gerecht, zum Beispiel für den unkomplizierten Auftritt auf Jobmessen. Aber das ist wieder eine andere Geschichte.

The Brand Box contains: a hinged counter, bar stools, clothes rails, screens and presentation boxes. The light pine wood together with the original scaffolding poles give the store the desired modern-urban look. Large digital screens convey the spirit of the brand and the latest campaign is presented on a 4D Magic Screen on an end wall.

The whole thing is also available on a smaller scale, to fit in a normal car, for example for an uncomplicated appearance at job fairs. But that's another story.

ANNEMARIE BÖRLIND
COSMETIC DISPLAY FAMILY

LOCATION GERMANY **CLIENT** BÖRLIND GMBH, CALW **CONCEPT / DESIGN** ARNO GMBH, WOLFSCHLUGEN
PHOTOGRAPHS PETER MUNTANION, REUTLINGEN

Um der wachsenden Nachfrage nach Naturkosmetik nachzukommen, entschloss sich das Familienunternehmen Börlind aus Calw im Schwarzwald bereits 2006, seine Produkte nicht nur in klassischen Reformhäusern, sondern auch in Parfümerien, Apotheken und Bioläden sowie ausgewählten Drogeriemärkten und Kaufhäusern anzubieten. Hierfür entwickelten die Retail Designer von ARNO in enger Zusammenarbeit mit dem Unternehmen eine neue Kosmetiktheke sowie den neuen General Tester Stand (GTS).

To meet the growing demand for natural cosmetics, the family-owned business Börlind from Calw in the Black Forest decided back in 2006 to sell its products not only in conventional health food stores, but also in perfumeries, pharmacies and stores specialising in organic products as well as selected drugstores and department stores. For these outlets, ARNO's retail designers worked closely with the company to develop a new cosmetics counter and the new General Tester Stand (GTS).

The brand's values and closeness to nature are underlined by the combination of plain white with subtle solid lime wood accents and a special lighting design. The product range is now clearly presented in easy-to-read units for both customers and sales staff. The functional design also makes it simple to replace haptic elements with digital components that are displayed on screen. Practical details such as the fold-down text bar for scannable codes and a drawer for storage keep the counter efficient and well organised. The GTS can be used as a table-top or free-standing display, depending on the location. In terms of the technical design, particular attention was paid to tipping stability, which was extensively tested with prototypes and optimised during the development process.

Die Werte und die Naturverbundenheit der Marke werden durch die Kombination aus schlichtem Weiß mit dezenten Massivholz-Highlights aus Linde und einer besonderen Lichtinszenierung unterstrichen. Die neue Gliederung in ablesbare Einheiten bietet sowohl für die Kundschaft als auch das Verkaufspersonal eine übersichtliche Präsentation der Produktpalette. Gleichzeitig ermöglicht die funktionale Gestaltung den einfachen Austausch von haptischen Elementen durch digitale Komponenten, die per Screen angezeigt werden. Praktische Details wie eine klappbare Textleiste für scanbare Codes und eine Depotschublade für Stauraum machen die Theke effizient und durchdacht. Der GTS kann je nach Einsatzort als Tisch- oder frei stehendes Display genutzt werden. Im Rahmen des technischen Designs wurde besonderes Augenmerk auf die Kippsicherheit gelegt, die anhand von Prototypen ausgiebig getestet und so im Entwicklungsprozess optimiert wurde.

In Zeiten, in denen Nachhaltigkeit und Umweltbewusstsein immer stärker in den Fokus rücken, gewinnt die Marke weiter an Bedeutung. Die Geschwister Alicia und Nicolas Lindner führen das Unternehmen in dritter Generation und legen großen Wert auf die Verbundenheit von Mensch und Natur. Die Entwicklung und Einführung neuer Retail Displays war ein logischer Schritt für das CSE-(Certified Sustainable Economics-)zertifizierte Unternehmen. Mit diesen Richtlinien werden nicht nur die Produkte, sondern das gesamte Unternehmen und dessen soziale und ökologische Grundhaltung überprüft.

In times when sustainability and environmental awareness are becoming increasingly important, the brand is gaining in significance. Siblings Alicia and Nicolas Lindner are the third generation of the family to run the business and are passionate about the connection between people and nature. The development and launch of new retail displays was a logical step for the CSE (Certified Sustainable Economics) certified company. These guidelines not only inspect the products, but also the entire company and its fundamental social and ecological stance.

EDEKA HAFENMARKT STROETMANN

LOCATION MÜNSTER, GERMANY **CLIENT** EDEKA HAFENMARKT STROETMANN, MÜNSTER
CONCEPT / DESIGN / GRAPHICS INTERSTORE AG, ZURICH **LIGHTING** IMOON LIGHTING LTD., MILAN
OTHERS SCHWEITZER PROJECT AG, NATURNS (SHOPFITTING) **PHOTOGRAPHS** DANIEL HORN PHOTOGRAPHY, BERLIN

Die Unternehmensgruppe L. Stroetmann ist ein in sechster Generation geführtes Familienunternehmen und betreibt mit 1.700 Mitarbeitenden deutschlandweit insgesamt zwanzig Standorte. Im Rahmen der Erschließung des Hafenviertels im Nordrhein-Westfälischen Münster hat sich die Gelegenheit geboten, einen neuen Lebensmittelmarkt mit einer ganz besonderen Atmosphäre zu bauen.

Die Aufgabenstellung für die Schweitzer Project AG aus Naturns in Südtirol bestand in der Realisierung eines authentischen Hafenmarkts, der sich harmonisch in die Nachbarschaft einer regen Restaurant- und Kneipenszene einfügt und gleichzeitig als Nahversorger für die Einwohner von Münster dient.

The L. Stroetmann Group is a sixth-generation family business with 1,700 employees and a total of twenty stores dotted around Germany. As part of the development of the harbour district in Münster, North Rhine-Westphalia, the opportunity arose to build a new grocery store with a very special atmosphere.

Schweitzer Project AG from Naturns in South Tyrol was tasked with creating an authentic harbour market that blends harmoniously into the lively neighbourhood of restaurants and pubs while at the same time serving as a local supplier for the people of Münster.

Passend zum Standort befindet sich im Eingangsbereich ein ausgedehnter Marktplatz mit diversen Gastronomieangeboten: ein Treffpunkt zum Plaudern, für den schnellen Einkauf, einen Kaffee oder ein Mittagessen zwischendurch. Die Farbpalette ist gekennzeichnet von einer ruhigen Grundtonalität in Grau mit markanten Farbakzenten in Blau, Weiß und Rot. In das maritime Thema wurde auch die Parkebene miteinbezogen, sodass sich der Kundschaft die Gestaltung des Marktes bereits in der Phase des Eintritts erschließt.

In keeping with the location, there is a large marketplace in the entrance area with a variety of eateries: a meeting place for a chat, a quick shop, a cup of coffee or a bite for lunch. The colour palette is characterised by a calm base of grey with bold splashes of blue, white and red. The parking level was also incorporated into the nautical theme, capturing the design for customers as soon as they enter the shopping centre.

Die Eigenständigkeit der Konzessionäre sorgt mit individuellem Retail Design, teilweise in Containeroptik mit Trapezblech und in markanten Farben, unterstützt von der jeweiligen Materialauswahl für ein vielfältiges Erscheinungsbild. Die Weinabteilung bildet mit einem von Schweitzer restaurierten authentischen Schrank eine Hommage an eine Münsteraner Institution: die ehemalige Spirituosenhandlung Hassenkamp. Im hinteren Bereich der Fläche erstrecken sich die Frischebereiche, deren Abteilungsbeschriftungen mit hinterleuchteten Buchstaben sowie auffallenden Leuchtelementen in Kombination mit Holzverkleidungen aus Astfichte für Orientierung sorgen.

The independence of the retailers ensures a diverse appearance, each with their own retail design, some in container look with trapezoidal sheet metal and in striking colours, supported by the choice of materials. With an authentic cabinet restored by Schweitzer, the wine section pays homage to a Münster institution: the former Hassenkamp liquour store. At the rear of the space are the fresh food departments, with signage of backlit letters and eye-catching lighting elements combined with knotty sprucewood panelling to help customers find their way around.

Die lokaltypische Backsteinoptik wird von einem erfrischenden Grafikkonzept aus der Feder von Interstore ergänzt. Die Retail-Agentur mit Hauptsitz in Zürich und Schwesterunternehmen von Schweitzer brachte ihre Kompetenzen vom Store Design über Visual Merchandising bis hin zum Grafikdesign ein. So heben aufgedruckte Boden- sowie maritime Wandgrafiken das Hafen- und Industriehallenthema weiter hervor. Auch Leuchtelemente in den Frischebereichen unterstreichen den inklusiven Markt-Claim „Mein Hafen – Mein Markt".

The typical local red-brick look is complemented by a refreshing graphic concept by Interstore. The Zurich-based retail agency and sister company of Schweitzer contributed its expertise in store design, through to visual merchandising and graphic design. Printed floor and maritime wall graphics further emphasise the port and industrial theme. Lighting elements in the fresh food areas also underline the overarching store claim "My Harbour – My Store".

BETTENRID

LOCATION MUNICH, GERMANY **CLIENT** BETTENRID, MUNICH **CONCEPT / DESIGN** UMDASCH THE STORE MAKERS, AMSTETTEN **PHOTOGRAPHS** JENS PFISTERER, STUTTGART

Zwei starke Frauen prägten die bewegte Unternehmensgeschichte des Münchner Textilunternehmens Bettenrid. Hedwig Rid, die 1929 ein kleines, auf die Reinigung von Bettfedern spezialisiertes Geschäft von Ihrer Mutter Rosa übernahm, legte den Grundstein für eine bayerische Erfolgsgeschichte im Einzelhandel.

Two strong women shaped the eventful history of the Munich-based textile company Bettenrid. Hedwig Rid, who took over a small shop specialising in cleaning duvet feathers from her mother Rosa in 1929, laid the foundations for a Bavarian success story in the retail sector.

Im Oktober 2023 eröffnete das komplett neu gestaltete erste Obergeschoss in der Theatinerstraße in München. Im Rahmen des Masterkonzepts von umdasch The Store Makers wurden seit 2018 alle vier Etagen des bayerischen Traditionsunternehmens für hochwertige Heimtextilien im Stil einer Altbauvilla umgebaut. Im Rahmen ihres „One-Stop-Shop" Ansatzes waren die Ladenbauer aus Amstetten in Niederösterreich für Konzept, Design und Planung, Möbel- und Ladenbau sowie General Contracting des gesamten Hauses verantwortlich.

Die rund 400 Quadratmeter Verkaufsfläche präsentieren sich mit vielen Details im Charme einer gediegenen Altbauvilla. So ziehen sich zum Beispiel Fischgrätparkett, Wandvertäfelungen und passende Einbauregale durch alle Etagen. Auch ein Welcome-Table mit stets frischem Blumenstrauß darf nicht fehlen. Ziel des langfristig angelegten Masterkonzepts war es, dass trotz der über mehrere Jahre verteilten Umbauarbeiten alles wie aus einem Guss wirkt.

The completely redesigned first floor on Theatinerstrasse in Munich opened in October 2023. As part of a master plan by umdasch The Store Makers', all four floors of the traditional Bavarian company for high-quality home textiles have been undergoing a transformation in the style of an old villa since 2018. As part of their "one-stop store" approach, the shopfitters from Amstetten in Lower Austria were responsible for the concept, design and planning, furniture and shopfitting as well as general contracting for the entire store.

The approximately 400 square meters of retail space is full of details that evoke the charm of a stately old villa. For example, herringbone parquet flooring, wall panelling and matching built-in shelves run through all the floors. A welcome table with a fresh bouquet of flowers is also a must. The aim of the long-term master plan was to ensure that, despite the renovation work being spread over several years, everything looked as if it had been cast from a single mould.

Das Herzstück im ersten Obergeschoss bildet „Rosa's Lounge", eine Coffeebar in Selbstbedienung. Die Lounge wurde im Stil einer Bibliothek mit gemütlichen Sitznischen gestaltet und ist geprägt von satten Grüntönen und üppigen Dschungelmomenten in Form von Tapeten. Um dem Thema Altbauvilla gerecht zu werden, integrierten die Gestaltenden viele traditionelle Einrichtungselemente: einen alten Waschtisch, einen dekorativen Kamin im Bereich der Wohndecken sowie einen altmodischen Herd und einen nachgebauten Buffetschrank in der Abteilung für Küchenwäsche. Als Signature Pieces sollen diese den „Sense of Place" der jeweiligen Sortimentsbereiche hervorheben.

The centrepiece on the second floor is "Rosa's Lounge", a self-service coffee bar. Designed in the style of a library with cosy seating niches, the lounge features lush greens and jungle touches in the form of wallpaper. In keeping with the old villa theme, the designers incorporated many traditional furnishing elements: an old washstand, a decorative fireplace in the sales area for living room throws as well as an old-fashioned stove and a replica buffet cabinet in the kitchen linen department. As signature pieces, these are intended to emphasise the 'sense of place' of the respective product ranges.

Der Einzelhandel und die Kompetenz der Mitarbeiterschaft lagen auch Günther Rid am Herzen, als er 1988 die Rid Stiftung für den bayerischen Einzelhandel gründete. Sein Credo, dass wirtschaftlicher Erfolg viel mit Kompetenzen zu tun hat und wenig mit der Größe eines Unternehmens, ist bis heute gültig.

Retailing and the expertise of its employees were also close to Günther Rid's heart when he set up the Rid Foundation for the Bavarian Retail Trade in 1988. His credo that economic success has a lot to do with skills and little to do with the size of a company is still valid today.

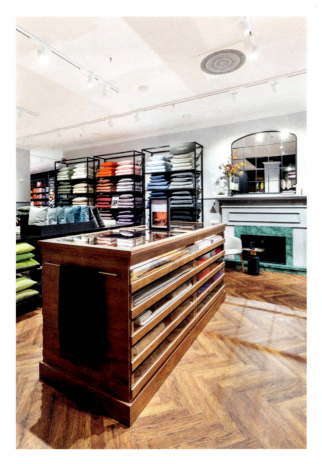

JEWELLERY PLETZSCH

LOCATION FRANKFURT AM MAIN, GERMANY   **CLIENT** JUWELIER PLETZSCH, FRANKFURT AM MAIN   **CONCEPT / DESIGN** HEIKAUS ARCHITEKTUR GMBH, STUTTGART   **GRAPHICS / LIGHTING** HEIKAUS ARCHITEKTUR GMBH, STUTTGART   **PHOTOGRAPHS** UWE SPOOERING, OHLENHARD

Weg von dunklem, schwerem Mobiliar und drückenden Strukturtapeten hin zu Exklusivität, Brillanz und Leichtigkeit. Das neue Designkonzept für Juwelier Pletzsch schafft Weite und Großzügigkeit in den bestehenden Räumlichkeiten auf der mondänen Frankfurter Zeil. Das Traditionshaus gilt als erste Adresse für Trauringe, Schmuck, Diamanten und Uhren. Das 120 Quadratmeter große Ladenlokal mit Meisterwerkstatt sollte vollständig umgebaut werden und künftig sowohl die Stammkundschaft als auch das jüngere Publikum ansprechen.

Away from dark, heavy furniture and oppressive textured wallpaper and towards exclusivity, brilliance and lightness. The new design concept for Jewellery Pletzsch creates a generous space in the existing premises on Frankfurt's fashionable Zeil shopping street. The traditional store is the first port of call for wedding rings, jewellery, diamonds and watches. The 120-square-metre premises, which include a master workshop, were to be completely renovated to appeal to both regular customers and a younger clientele.

In einem Zeitraum von nur acht Wochen mussten das gesamte Bestandsmobiliar sowie der Bodenbelag und Deckenkonstruktionen demontiert werden. Die Nachbargeschäfte wie auch die Kundschaft sollten möglichst wenig Einschränkungen durch den Umbau erfahren. Eine enorme Herausforderung für das Team der Heikaus-Gruppe, die seit 1992 schlüsselfertige Innenausbauten plant und realisiert. Sowohl die Abrissarbeiten mit Entsorgung als auch die Anlieferung galt es sauber und diskret durchzuführen – nebst allen erforderlichen Gewerken wie Bodenlegen, Trocken-, Ladenbau, Elektrik und Malerarbeiten. Zudem mussten die hohen Sicherheitsstandards zur Präsentation der wertvollen Schmuckstücke sowie hochwertigen Uhren in das Gestaltungskonzept integriert werden.

All the existing furniture, flooring and ceiling structures had to be removed in just eight weeks. Neighbouring stores and customers were to be affected as little as possible. An enormous challenge for the team from the Heikaus Group, who have been planning and implementing turnkey interior fittings since 1992. Both the demolition work, including disposal, and the delivery had to be carried out cleanly and discreetly – in addition to all the necessary trades such as floor laying, drywall, shopfitting, electrics and painting. On top of that, the high security standards for the presentation of the valuable pieces of jewellery and high-end watches had to be integrated into the design concept.

The warm wood-look flooring, laid in a herringbone pattern, creates a bright and light-flooded sales area reminiscent of a festive ballroom. Velvet curtains, wall elements and central room furniture in a white marble finish, flanked by brass-framed mirrors and display cabinets, reinforce this impression. Privacy and discreet consultation areas are created by elevated, floating jewellery showcases with ceiling connections and fluffy carpet islands, which are formally reflected in the ceiling design. The high-quality jewellery is displayed exclusively on recessed leather surfaces in the display shelves and consultation tables.

Mit dem warmen Bodenbelag in Holzoptik, verlegt im Fischgrätverbund, erinnert die helle und lichtdurchflutete Verkaufsfläche an einen feierlichen Ballsaal. Samtvorhänge, Wandelemente sowie Mittelraummöbel in weißer Marmoroptik, flankiert von in Messing eingefassten Spiegeln und Vitrinen, unterstreichen diesen Eindruck. Privatsphäre und diskrete Beratungsbereiche entstehen durch aufgeständerte, schwebend wirkende Schmuckvitrinen mit Deckenverbindung sowie flauschige Teppichinseln, die sich in der Deckengestaltung formal widerspiegeln. Die hochwertigen Schmuckstücke werden exklusiv auf eingelassenen Lederflächen in den Vitrinenböden und Beratungstischen präsentiert.

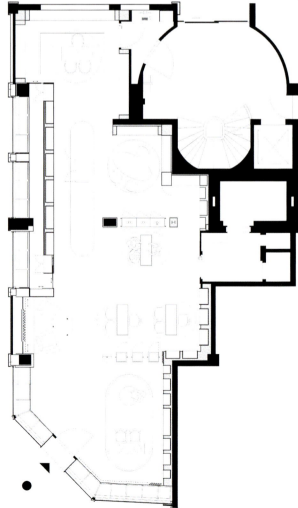

POGGENPOHL SHANGHAI EXPERIENCE CENTER

LOCATION SHANGHAI, CHINA **CLIENT** POGGENPOHL MANUFACTURING GMBH, HERFORD **CONCEPT / DESIGN** IPPOLITO FLEITZ GROUP – IDENTITY ARCHITECTS, STUTTGART **LIGHTING** ADDING PLUME LIGHTING DESIGN SHANGHAI CO., LTD. (CONSULTANT) **PHOTOGRAPHS** ZHU DI, SHANGHAI

Die Küche ist der zentrale Ort im Alltag vieler Menschen. Hier kommen wir zusammen, hier nehmen wir uns Zeit füreinander, für Austausch und gemeinsamen Genuss. Jeder weiß: In der Küche ist die Party am schönsten. Die Schlüsselfigur des neuen Experience Center für Poggenpohl ist deshalb ein großer Tisch im Zentrum des Raumes. Von hier aus wird die Bedeutung der Küche nicht nur funktional, sondern auch emotional aufgespannt. Alle kommen an einen Tisch – die Küche als Ort der Kommunikation und Community.

The kitchen is the central place in many people's daily lives. It is where we meet up, where we take time for each other, where we chat and where we eat and drink together. As everyone knows: The kitchen is where the party is! The central feature of the new Experience Center for Poggenpohl is therefore a large table in the middle of the room. From here, it becomes clear that the kitchen is not just functional, but also emotional. Everyone gathers around the table – the kitchen as a place of communication and community.

Poggenpohl steht für moderne Küchen mit höchsten Qualitätsansprüchen und Handwerkskunst „made in Germany". 2022 eröffnete im Herzen Shanghais das Poggenpohl Experience Center nach dem Entwurf der Ippolito Fleitz Group GmbH mit Sitz in Stuttgart und Filialen unter anderem auch in Shanghai: „Wir gestalten den Showroom als hybriden Raum, der zeitgemäßes Retail Design erlebbar macht. Das Experience Center ist weder toter Ausstellungsraum noch dröge Verkaufsfläche, sondern ein lebendiger, multiperspektivischer Erfahrungsraum, der zum Entdecken, Probieren und Teilen einlädt".

Diesem Leitmotiv folgend ist das Experience Center hybrid gestaltet, als Ort, der das Zusammenkommen und das gemeinsame Erleben in den Mittelpunkt stellt. So steht der große Tisch mit seiner mächtigen Platte auf Rollen – der Raum kann somit in allen Facetten bespielt werden. Vom Kochevent über Produktpräsentationen bis hin zur Modenschau ist alles möglich.

Poggenpohl stands for modern kitchens of the highest quality and craftsmanship "made in Germany". In 2022, the Poggenpohl Experience Center opened in the heart of Shanghai. It was designed by Stuttgart-based Ippolito Fleitz Group GmbH, which also has a branch in Shanghai: "We design showrooms as hybrid spaces that bring contemporary retail design to life. The Experience Center is neither a dead exhibition space nor a dull shop floor, but a lively, multi-perspective experience space that invites you to discover, try out and share.

Following this leitmotif, the Experience Center is designed as a place with a hybrid nature, one that focuses on people coming together and enjoying shared experiences. The large table with its massive top is mounted on castors, allowing the space to be used in all its facets. From cooking events and product presentations to fashion shows, everything is possible.

In den Showroom integriert ist außerdem ein öffentlich zugängliches Café mit eigener Terrasse, das vollständig mit Poggenpohl-Küchenmodulen ausgestattet ist. Die Gestalter haben keine harten Begrenzungen durch Wände vorgesehen, sondern schaffen stattdessen einen offenen, fließenden Raum. Mit der Bespielung der Decken wurde dennoch eine Zonierung angedeutet.

Bereits das Foyer empfängt die Besucherschaft mit einer abgehängten Installation getrockneter Pflanzen. Hinter grün bemalten Bögen springt die Decke aus kunstvoll geflochtenem Rattan ins Auge. Der Werkstoff, der aus der dafür berühmten Provinz Zhejiang stammt, überspannt das Material Lab.

Also integrated into the showroom is a public café with its own terrace, which is fully equipped with Poggenpohl kitchen modules. Rather than creating boundaries with walls, the designers have created an open, flowing location. The design of the ceilings does, however, suggest some zoning.

The foyer welcomes visitors with a suspended installation of dried plants. Behind green-painted arches, a ceiling made of artfully woven rattan catches the eye. This material, which comes from the famous Zhejiang province, spans the Material Lab.

SPACES   POGGENPOHL SHANGHAI EXPERIENCE CENTER

Die moderne Küche vereint zwei Themen: Sie ist einerseits hochtechnisch und andererseits mit den Zutaten ganz in der Natur. Technische Innovation und Smart Home treffen auf das Bedürfnis nach einem gesunden Lebensstil und der Sehnsucht nach Naturverbundenheit.

The modern kitchen combines two themes: On the one hand, it is high-tech and, on the other, the ingredients are completely natural. Technical innovation and smart homes meet the need for a healthy lifestyle and the desire to be close to nature.

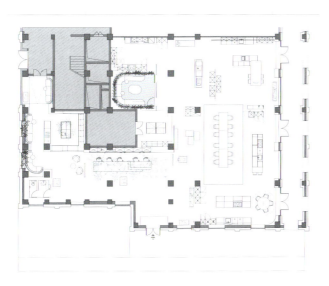

MELT SEASON FLAGSHIP AT TAIYUAN ROAD

LOCATION SHANGHAI, CHINA **CLIENT** MELT SEASON, VERSE CHINA, SHANGHAI **CONCEPT / DESIGN** MLKK STUDIO LIMITED, HONG KONG **PHOTOGRAPHS** WONG KE, SHANGHAI

Melt Season, eine hochwertige neue orientalische Parfümmarke, hat seinen ersten Flagshipstore in Shanghai eröffnet. Nach dem Credo des Gründers ist das sinnliche Erleben ganz an den gegebenen olfaktorischen Eindruck gebunden, in dem Selbsterfahrung, Widerspruch und Harmonie koexistieren. Der Flagship-Pilot der Marke befindet sich an der Taiyuan Road, bekannt als frühere Residenz von Cheng Nien, dem „letzten Socialite von Shanghai".

Melt Season, a new oriental speciality perfume brand, has opened its first flagship store in Shanghai. The founder believes that the senses focus on the present olfactory experience, where self-awareness, contradiction, and harmony coexist. The brand's pilot flagship store is located on Taiyuan Road, famous for being the former residence of Cheng Nien, known as the "last socialite of Shanghai".

Das mit dem Design beauftragte Architekturbüro Mlkk Studio wurde 2016 von den drei Architekten Mavis Yip, Kian Yam und Kwanho Li in Hongkong gegründet, die sich seither einer Architektur für das Gemeinwohl verschrieben haben. Nach acht Monaten intensiver Vor-Ort-Recherche auf dem historischen Terrain hat das Team letztlich das jetzige denkmalgeschützte Gebäude für den Einbau des Stores gewählt. Nicht nur ist es praktischerweise nahe der Straße gelegen, es verströmt auch das beruhigende Flair, das für olfaktorische Erlebnisse den idealen Rahmen bildet.

The architectural studio entrusted with the design, Mlkk Studio, was founded in Hong Kong in 2016 by the three architects, Mavis Yip, Kian Yam, and Kwanho Li, who have since then dedicated themselves to creating architecture for the public good. After eight months of extensive on-site research in the conservation area, the team finally chose this site in a historically preserved building. Not only is it conveniently located close to the street, but it also has a tranquil ambience that is ideal for creating olfactory experiences.

The retail design aims to continue the historical and cultural context of old Shanghai. The redesign preserves six towering Chinese water pine trees in the courtyard of the Spanish-style garden villa. At the entrance, a white "picture frame" acts as a garden-style partition, creating an interplay between the interior and exterior. The ground floor is designed to be flexible. Micro-cement connects the ceiling, façade, and floor, creating an intriguing atmosphere akin to a primitive cave. After walking through the passage and up the stairs, visitors are greeted by a bright and refreshing space. In contrast to the ground floor, this area feels clearer and more transparent.

Mit dem Retail Design will man den historischen und kulturellen Kontext des alten Shanghai fortführen. Die Neugestaltung bezieht im Hof der im spanischen Stil gehaltenen Gartenvilla sechs mächtige chinesische Latschenkiefern mit ein. Am Eingang fungiert ein zum Garten passender weißer „Bilderrahmen" als Trennelement und schafft ein Wechselspiel zwischen innen und außen. Das Erdgeschoss wurde flexibel gestaltet. Hier erzeugen Decke, Fassade und Boden, durch Mikrozement miteinander verbunden, eine reizvolle Stimmung, die an das Innere einer Höhle erinnert. Nach dem Gang durch den Flur und die Treppe hinauf werden Besuchende von einem erfrischend farbenfrohen Raum empfangen. Im Gegensatz zum Erdgeschoss ist dieser Bereich heller und transparenter gestaltet.

Im Obergeschoss schließlich hat Mlkk Studio die originale hölzerne Dachstruktur des denkmalgeschützten Gebäudes restauriert. Auch hier wurden die Wände kunstvoll mit Mikrozement verkleidet. Im Herzen des Raums betont ein Materialwechsel die Form des Präsentationstresens: Zum Blickfang werden polierte natürliche Sandsteinplatten, über denen die Produkte arrangiert sind. Die zum Farbschema passenden abgehängten Leuchten variieren in der Höhe, sodass sie das Warenangebot effektvoll illuminieren.

Ein Zusammenspiel zwischen Düften, Architektur und Natur lässt einen elegant-poetischen Raum entstehen – so die fernöstlich inspirierte Interpretation der Marke und der Gestaltenden. Einen Raum, der die Balance der Beziehung zwischen Menschen, Objekten und der Natur einfängt.

On the upper floor, Mlkk Studio has restored the original timber roof structure of the listed building. Here too, the micro-cement craftsmanship has been applied to the walls. At the centre of the space, a change in materials emphasises the shape of the display counter: Polished natural sandstone slabs become the visual focal point, with products arranged above them. Pendant lights in the same colour scheme vary in height, effectively illuminating the product area.

Fragrance, architecture and nature intertwine here to create an elegant and poetic space. This is the Eastern conceptual interpretation of the brand and the design team, balancing the relationship between people, objects, and nature within the space.

NIO HOUSE DUSSELDORF

LOCATION DUSSELDORF, GERMANY **CLIENT** NIO DEUTSCHLAND GMBH, GRÄFELFING **CONCEPT / DESIGN** SHL – SCHMIDT HAMMER LASSEN, COPENHAGEN **OTHERS** VIZONA GMBH, WEIL AM RHEIN (PROJECT MANAGEMENT / GENERAL CONTRACTING / SHOPFITTING) **PHOTOGRAPHS** ROMAN THOMAS, CELLE

An der Schnittstelle zur Kundschaft bieten die NIO Houses neben Präsentationsflächen auch Raum für Veranstaltungen, die nicht unmittelbar mit Elektromobilität zu tun haben. Mit Café, Konferenzbereich, Children's Hub und Coworking-Räumen ist der Standort in Düsseldorf als Ort für Kultur und Begegnung im Herzen der Rheinmetropole gedacht.

Die Ausführung des neuen Retail Designs und des Markenansatzes verantwortete Vizona als Generalunternehmer. Der Standort in stark frequentierter Einkaufslage der Innenstadt unterlag streng regulierten Anforderungen an zeitgenaue Lieferungen mit wenig Platz für Material und vielfachem Umschichten.

At the interface with customers, the NIO Houses offer presentation areas as well as space for events that are not directly related to electromobility. With a café, conference area, children's hub and co-working spaces, the location in Dusseldorf is designed as a place for culture and encounters at the heart of the Rhine metropolis.

As general contractor, Vizona was responsible for the implementation of the new retail design and the brand image. The location in a highly frequented shopping area in the city centre was subject to strictly regulated requirements for precisely scheduled deliveries with little space for materials and multiple rearrangements.

SPACES   NIO HOUSE DUSSELDORF

It took eight months of construction from commissioning to opening to create an elegant open space of around 1,200 square metres on three levels, with no thresholds to impede entry or exit. Over three floors, convex fluted concrete walls and seamlessly joined ash wood panelling frame the walkways of visitors from the e-community.

In 8 Monaten Bauzeit von der Beauftragung bis zu Eröffnung ist auf rund 1.200 Quadratmetern und 3 Ebenen ein eleganter Open Space entstanden, der ohne Schwellenangst betreten, aber auch wieder verlassen werden kann. Über drei Etagen rahmen konvex kannelierte Betonwände und fugengenau angeschlossene Verkleidungen aus Eschenholz die Laufwege der interessierten E-Community.

Zahlreiche Sonderanfertigungen, wie die Filzlamellen an der Decke und Lichtfelder mit einer Größe bis zu 50 Quadratmetern im UG, verlangten eine besondere Detaillierung. Die komplexe digitale Hardware, unter anderem mit großen LED-Bildschirmflächen, Zutrittskontrollen und Content via Fernzugriff, wurde bereits im Vorfeld der Elektroplanung berücksichtigt. In Zusammenarbeit mit dem skandinavischen Architekturbüro SHL – Schmidt Hammer Lassen Architects sind aktuell weitere Standorte in Planung.

Numerous bespoke features, such as the felt lamella on the ceiling and light panels of up to 50 square metres in size in the basement, required special attention to detail. The complex digital hardware, including large LED screens, access control and content via remote access, was already taken into account in the preliminary stages of the electrical planning. Other locations are currently being planned in collaboration with the Scandinavian SHL – Schmidt Hammer Lassen Architects.

SPACES   NIO HOUSE DUSSELDORF

The name Nio means "blue sky coming" in Chinese characters and encapsulates the corporate vision to change the future of our planet sustainably by taking progressive action. Founded in China in 2014, the provider of electric mobility concepts entered the markets in Denmark, Sweden, the Netherlands and Germany in 2022 following its launch in Oslo, Norway. In addition to the group's design centre in Munich, the company operates the Berlin Innovation Center for autonomous driving, digital cockpit and energy research.

Der Name Nio bedeutet in chinesischen Schriftzeichen „Der Himmel wird blau" und verkörpert die unternehmenseigene Vision, die Zukunft unseres Planeten durch progressives Handeln nachhaltig zu verändern. 2014 in China gegründet, folgte nach dem Auftakt im norwegischen Oslo 2022 der Markteintritt des Anbieters von Elektromobilitätskonzepten in Dänemark, Schweden, den Niederlanden und Deutschland. Neben dem Designzentrum des Konzerns in München betreibt das Unternehmen das Berliner Innovationszentrum für autonomes Fahren, digitales Cockpit und Energieforschung.

SV DARMSTADT 98

LOCATION DARMSTADT, GERMANY   **CLIENT** SV DARMSTADT 1898 E.V., DARMSTADT
CONCEPT / DESIGN CBA CLEMENS BACHMANN ARCHITEKTEN, MUNICH   **PHOTOGRAPHS** BERND DUCKE, OTTOBRUNN

Aufgrund der Lilie im Vereinslogo wird der Sportverein Darmstadt 1898 e.V. – kurz SV Darmstadt 98 – auch „Die Lilien" genannt. Seit Juli 2012 sind zudem alle sozialen Aktionen des SV 98 unter dem Namen „Im Zeichen der Lilie" gebündelt. Die Lilien sind fest im Profifußball verankert, auch durch den sukzessiven Umbau des heutigen Merck-Stadions. Der Club-CI der Lilien folgend ziehen sich die Farben Weiß und Blau im Wechsel durch nahezu alle Bereiche des auch als „Bölle" bekannten Stadions am Böllenfalltor.

Because of the lily in the club logo, Sportverein Darmstadt 1898 e.V. – SV Darmstadt 98 for short – is also known as 'The Lilies'. Since July 2012, all of SV 98's social activities have also been bundled "In the Sign of the Lily". The Lilies are firmly anchored in professional football, thanks in part to the successive conversions of what is now Merck Stadium. In keeping with the CI of the Lilies' club, the colours white and blue alternate through almost all areas of the stadium at Böllenfalltor, also referred to affectionately as the 'Bölle'.

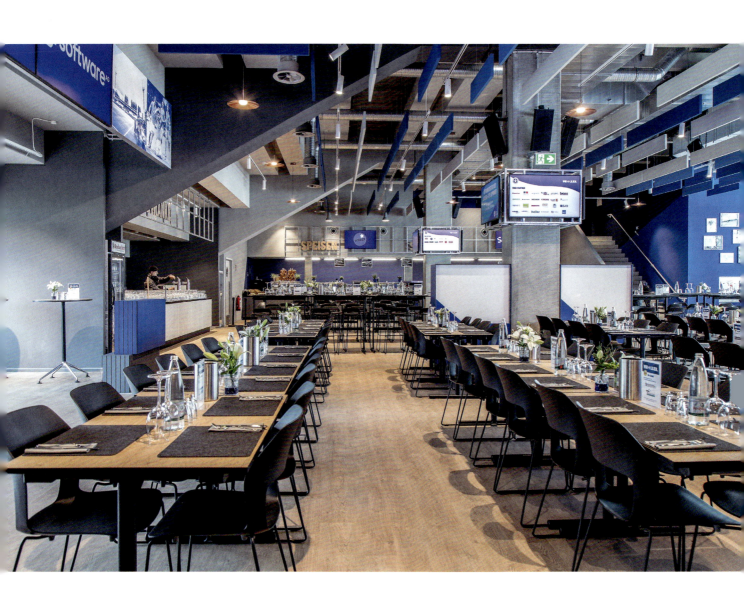

Im Zuge des Neubaus der Stadion-Haupttribüne wurden CBA Clemens Bachmann Architekten damit beauftragt, die neuen Hospitalityflächen sowie Funktions- und Nebenräume auf drei Ebenen zu gestalten. Gewünscht wurde ein Interior Design mit hohem Wiedererkennungswert und großer Vereinsidentifikation. Die symmetrisch aufgebaute, größte Fläche im Erdgeschoss erhielt eine zentrale Bar als zukünftige Anlaufstelle aller Gäste vor und nach dem Spiel. Von diesem blauen Kern aus wurden blau-weiße Akustikelemente an der Decke linear in die Sitzbereiche sowie an die Zu- und Ausgänge geführt.

CBA Clemens Bachmann Architekten were commissioned to design the new hospitality areas as well as functional and ancillary rooms on three levels as part of the new construction of the main stand. The brief was to create an interior design with a high recognition factor and strong club identification. The symmetrically structured, largest area on the ground floor was given a central bar as a future meeting point for all guests before and after the match. From this blue core, blue and white acoustic elements were drawn in lines on the ceiling into the seating areas and towards the entrances and exits.

Dieses Gestaltungsmerkmal wird im Obergeschoss aufgegriffen und schafft so eine Verbindung zwischen den Ebenen. Orange ist als Komplementärfarbton dem intensiven Blau entgegengesetzt. Die reflektierenden metallischen Einbauten und Oberflächen in Kupfer schaffen einen warmen, atmosphärischen Akzent und das strukturierte Holz des Bodens sowie der Tische wirkt gemütlich und einladend. Die Ausgabetheken wurden einheitlich gestaltet – sie unterscheiden sich lediglich in der Farbgebung der Verkleidungen. Die Nebenräume im Untergeschoss wie Umkleidekabine, Mixed Zone und der Pressebereich sind gemäß dem Selbstverständnis des Clubs bewusst zurückhaltend und einfach gehalten. Hier liegt der Fokus auf dem Wesentlichen: Fußball, Team Spirit, Emotion und Tradition. Blaue, polygonale Wandflächen schaffen dynamische Rauminszenierungen. So wurden in der Heimumkleide alle Funktionen entlang der Wände in einheitlichen Blautönen gestaltet.

This design feature is repeated on the upper floor, creating a connection between the levels. Orange is the complementary colour to the intense blue. The reflective metallic fixtures and copper surfaces create a warm, atmospheric accent and the textured wood of the floor and tables is cosy and inviting. The serving counters have a uniform design, only the colour of the panels varies. The ancillary areas in the basement, such as the changing rooms, mixed zone and press area, are deliberately understated and simple, in keeping with the club's self-image. The focus here is on the essentials: football, team spirit, emotion and tradition. Blue, polygonal wall surfaces create dynamic spaces. In the home changing room, for example, all the functions along the walls have been designed in uniform shades of blue.

Die Wände des Spielertunnels säumen die Namen von Unterstützern, Fans und Kooperationspartnern. Als authentische Reminiszenz an das ehemalige Stadion am Böllenfalltor dienen auf den Flächen alte, originale Stahlwellenbrecher der Tribüne als Raumteiler.

The walls of the players' tunnel are lined with the names of supporters, fans and cooperation partners. As an authentic reminder of the former stadium at Böllenfalltor, old, original steel wave breakers from the stands serve as partitions.

QUADFLIEG

LOCATION ARNSBERG, GERMANY   **CLIENT** QUADFLIEG GMBH & CO. KG, ARNSBERG
CONCEPT / DESIGN THEODOR SCHEMBERG EINRICHTUNGEN GMBH, METTINGEN   **PHOTOGRAPHS** REINHARD ROSENDAHL FOTOGRAFIE, VAREL

Der Anteil an Fahrrädern im Straßenbild hat sich in den letzten Jahren gefühlt deutlich vervielfacht. Die Corona-Pandemie, neue Leasingmodelle wie das Jobrad und technische Innovation haben der Branche einen deutlichen Nachfrageschub beschert. Mit diesem Rückenwind wollte Quadflieg ein neues Gebäude in Arnsberg errichten, um dort sein Fahrradparadies zu verwirklichen. Doch nach intensiver Suche entschied sich das Unternehmen für die Revitalisierung einer schon bestehenden Immobilie, um nachhaltig und ressourcenschonend zu investieren.

It seems that the number of bicycles on the road has significantly multiplied in recent years. The coronavirus pandemic, new leasing models such as the job bike and technical innovations have given the industry a significant boost in demand. With this tailwind, Quadflieg wanted to erect a new building in Arnsberg to house its bicycle paradise. However, after an intensive search, the company decided to revitalise an existing property in order to make a sustainable and resource-saving investment.

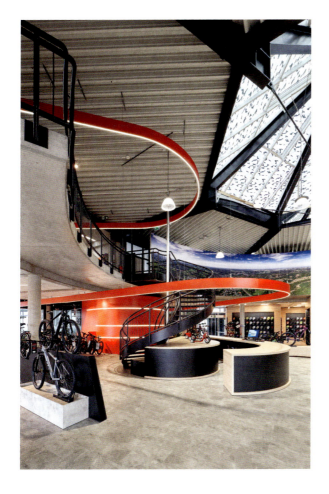

Die komplett runde Gebäudeform war planerisch eine besondere Herausforderung. Mit Schemberg beauftragten die Inhaber Dustin Brondke und Carsten Vornweg einen erfahrenen Ladenbauexperten für Fahrrad-Shopeinrichtungen. Das in die Jahre gekommene Bestandsgebäude diente einst als Autohaus, später als Fitnessstudio und stand dann lange Zeit leer. Möglichst viele Elemente, die bauseitig vorhanden waren, wurden aufbereitet und ins Konzept integriert.

Warme Holztöne und puristische Betonflächen schaffen eine einladende Atmosphäre, während das markante Rot, die Markenfarbe Quadfliegs, durch verschiedene Elemente im gesamten Laden präsent ist: von der weitläufigen Ausstellungsfläche im Untergeschoss – mit kleiner Spielecke für Kinder und Café-Lounge für die erwachsene Kundschaft – bis in die zweite Etage, die den Verkaufsbereich rund um das Thema Sicherheitstechnik beherbergt. Dabei war essenziell, dass die Kundenführung optimal durch den Store verläuft. Rote Lichtelemente dienen als visueller Ankerpunkt und lenken die Blicke der Kundschaft nach oben.

The completely circular shape of the building was a particular challenge during the planning phase. Owners Dustin Brondke and Carsten Vornweg turned to Schemberg, an experienced shopfitting expert for bicycle stores. The ageing existing building had once been a car dealership, then a gym and then stood empty for a long time. As many existing elements as possible were used and integrated into the concept.

Warm wood tones and purist concrete surfaces create an inviting atmosphere, while bold red, Quadflieg's brand colour, is present in various elements throughout the store: from the spacious product display areas on the ground floor – including a small play corner for children and the café lounge for adult customers – through to the second floor, where the security technology sales area is located. Having optimised customer navigation through the store was important. Red lighting elements serve as a visual anchor point, drawing customers' attention upwards.

In Anlehnung an die kreisförmige Architektur steht im Zentrum die runde Abholstation. Im großzügig bemessenen Innenraum können die Kund:innen Produkte auswählen und ausprobieren. Aber auch außerhalb des Ladens gibt es zukünftig die Möglichkeit, die Bikes unter Realbedingungen zu testen. Die Teststrecke beinhaltet verschiedene Pflastersorten, eine kleine Rampe und einen Hügel. Laut Aussage von Quadflieg „flanieren die Kunden nun durch den Laden und lassen sich von den Highlights inspirieren", was sich auch in gestiegenen Verkaufszahlen niederschlägt.

Based on the circular architecture, the round-shaped pick-up station is located in the centre. Customers can select and try out products in the spacious interior. In future, it will also be possible to test the bikes under real conditions outside the store. The test track includes different types of paving, a small ramp and a hill. According to Quadflieg, "customers now stroll through the store and are inspired by the highlights", which is reflected in increased sales.

GENESIS STUDIOS

LOCATION ZURICH / BASLE / GENEVA, SWITZERLAND / FRANKFURT AM MAIN, GERMANY **CLIENT** GENESIS MOTOR EUROPE GMBH, OFFENBACH AM MAIN **CONCEPT / DESIGN** SUH ARCHITECTS, SEOUL; MINT ARCHITECTURE, ZURICH, PART OF THE ATP GROUP **PHOTOGRAPHS** OLIVER RUST | KO GMBH, ZURICH; MIKEL PRIETO | MPK PHOTOS & FILMS, MADRID

„Unser Interior Design ist ruhig und reduziert, um das größtmögliche Gefühl individuellen Freiraums zu schaffen. Damit folgen wir dem Konzept der ‚Schönheit des weißen Raums', das von der koreanischen Architektur inspiriert ist", heißt es in der Designphilosophie der südkoreanischen Automarke Genesis. Zum Eintritt in den europäischen Markt wurde Mint Architecture mit der Planung und Realisation des ersten, als Flagship konzipierten Studios in der Schweiz an der Zürcher Bahnhofstrasse beauftragt.

"Our interior design is calm and minimalist in order to create the greatest possible sense of individual freedom. We follow the concept of the 'beauty of white space', which is inspired by Korean architecture," says the design philosophy of the South Korean car brand Genesis. To enable it to enter the European market, Mint Architecture was tasked with the design and build of the first flagship studio in Switzerland on Zurich's Bahnhofstrasse.

SPACES   GENESIS STUDIOS

Auf knapp 1.000 Quadratmetern entstand auf drei Etagen das erste Genesis Studio in der Schweiz mit Showroom, Loungebereich und eigenem Eventspace. Das Retail Design stammt von den koreanischen Architekten Suh Architects im Auftrag des Autokonzerns und beruht auf dem Anspruch, die Marke mit allen Sinnen zu erleben. Ausdruck dafür war ein Konzept, das hochwertige Materialien und modernste Technologie kombiniert und in Form von Kunstobjekten und Designinstallationen inszeniert. Mint Architecture übernahm die Gesamtplanung und rückte Inszenierungen und Materialisierung in den Mittelpunkt. In Zusammenarbeit mit lokalen Partnern entstanden Objekte, Installationen und Lösungen, die ausschließlich für das Zürcher Studio entwickelt wurden.

The first Genesis Studio in Switzerland with a showroom, lounge area and event space was created on three floors covering almost 1,000 square metres. The retail design was created by the Korean architects Suh Architects on behalf of the car manufacturer and is based on the claim that a brand should be experienced with all the senses. This is expressed in a concept that combines high-quality materials and state-of-the-art technology, staged in the form of objets d'art and design installations. Mint Architecture was responsible for the overall design and focused on staging and materialisation. In collaboration with local partners, objects, installations and solutions were developed exclusively for the Zurich studio.

Das Herzstück bildet ein aus 3.300 Kupferröhrchen bestehendes Kunstobjekt, das wie ein Baldachin über dem Eingang des Studios schwebt. Das Objekt wurde von Mint Architecture anhand der Visualisierung und der Materialität der südkoreanischen Architekten in Zusammenarbeit mit einem Südtiroler Stahlanbieter geplant und umgesetzt. Exemplarisch für die Materialwahl ist die kombinierte Gestaltung der Wände aus einer handgefertigten mineralischen Oberfläche in Sichtbeton-Ästhetik sowie einer Fläche aus Stahl. LED-basierte Multimedia-Installationen begleiten die Besuchenden auf allen drei Etagen und liefern den audiovisuellen Teppich für das Markenerlebnis. Die Inhalte können auf allen Stockwerken in gleicher Qualität und Lautstärke abgespielt werden.

The centrepiece is an objet d'art consisting of 3,300 copper tubes suspended like a canopy over the entrance to the studio. The creation was designed and realised by Mint Architecture based on the visualisation and materiality of the South Korean architects in collaboration with a South Tyrolean steel supplier. The combined design of the walls, consisting of a hand-finished mineral surface with an exposed concrete look and a steel surface, is an example of the choice of materials. LED-based multimedia installations accompany visitors on all three floors and provide the audiovisual backdrop for the brand experience. Content can be played on all floors in the same quality and volume.

„Getreu unserer Herkunft steht bei uns die koreanische Idee im Mittelpunkt, dass Sie mehr sind als ein Kunde. Wir behandeln Sie als unseren son-nim (손님), einen geschätzten Gast", beschreibt das Unternehmen seine Haltung gegenüber der Kundschaft. Nach dem Flagship Studio in Zürich konnte Mint Architecture als lokaler Architekt drei weitere Standorte in Europa planen und umsetzen.

"True to our heritage, our focus is on the Korean idea that you are more than just a customer. We treat you as our son-nim (손님), a valued guest," is how the company describes its attitude towards its customers. After the flagship studio in Zurich, Mint Architecture went on to design and implement three more locations in Europe as the local architect.

PUPPENKÖNIG

LOCATION BONN, GERMANY **CLIENT** PUPPENKÖNIG GMBH, BONN **CONCEPT / DESIGN** UMDASCH THE STORE MAKERS, AMSTETTEN **MEDIA** UMDASCH THE STORE MAKERS, AMSTETTEN (DIGITAL SIGNAGE, INTERACTIVE APPLICATIONS, SOFTWARE DEVELOPMENT) **PHOTOGRAPHS** JENS PFISTERER, STUTTGART

Das Spielwarengeschäft mit dem einprägsamen Namen Puppenkönig hat viele Generationen von Bonner „Pänz" und deren Eltern mit riesigen Modelleisenbahn-Landschaften begeistert. Nun weht auf den rund 800 Quadratmetern ein komplett neuer Wind, der den veränderten Bedürfnissen nach mehr Einkaufserlebnis mit „Gaming" und Events unter einem Dach entgegenkommt.

Neben der Planung und Umsetzung des gesamten Retail Designs mit aufwendigem Kulissenbau lag auch die Konzeption und Integration der digitalen Elemente in den Händen der umdasch Store Makers.

The toy store with the catchy name Puppenkönig (King of Dolls) has delighted many generations of kiddies and their parents in the city of Bonn with its huge model railroad landscapes. Now, the winds of change are blowing through the 800 square metres, meeting the changing demands for more shopping experience with gaming and events under one roof.

In addition to the planning and implementation of the entire retail design including elaborate scenery construction, the umdasch Store Makers were also responsible for the conception and integration of the digital elements.

SPACES PUPPENKÖNIG

The aim was to create a contemporary point of emotion together with the new owners. At its centre is an extensive landscape that is designed to invite interactive role-playing with life-size characters. The most popular Playmobil themes such as police, fire brigade, space and princess castle through to the world of knights serve as a backdrop.

Ziel war es, gemeinsam mit den neuen Inhabern einen zeitgemäßen „Point of Emotion" zu schaffen. In dessen Zentrum steht eine umfangreiche Kulissenlandschaft, die zum interaktiven Rollenspiel mit lebensgroßen Spielfiguren einladen soll. Als Kulisse dienen die beliebtesten Playmobil-Themen wie Polizei, Feuerwehr, Weltraum und Prinzessinnenschloss bis zur Ritterwelt.

Im Bereich „Wiltopia" warten Quizfragen und Rätsel zur Welt der Tiere und Pflanzen auf einem Touchscreen darauf, gelöst zu werden. Das Feenreich „Ayuma" kann mit einem Avatar erkundet werden, der mittels Sensoren die Bewegungen der Kinder wiedergibt. Auf einem anderen Screen können die kleinen Besucherinnen und Besucher als mutige Feuerwehrfrauen und -männer brennende Häuser mit einer haptischen Wasserpistole löschen und so spielerisch Punkte sammeln. Urzeitliche Abenteuer lassen sich in der Spielwelt „Dino Rise" erleben, in der die umdasch Digitalexperten mithilfe von Beamern eine audiovisuelle Animation erschufen. In einem weiteren Themenbereich können die Kinder in der Kulisse einer intergalaktischen Raumfahrtsmission per Touchscreen ein Raumschiff durchs All steuern und dabei verschiedene Aufgaben lösen. Zudem wurden eine Eventbühne und ein Bistro in das Konzept integriert.

Wo einst weihnachtlich geschmückte Schaufenster Kinderaugen zum Leuchten brachten, tut dies heute der Puppenkönig: als erlebnisorientierter Begegnungsort für Kids und ihre Begleitpersonen mitten in der Bonner Innenstadt.

In the Wiltopia area, touch-screen quizzes and puzzles about the world of animals and plants are waiting to be solved. The fairy kingdom of Ayuma can be explored with an avatar that uses sensors to mirror the children's movements. On another screen, young visitors can extinguish burning houses with a haptic water pistol as brave firefighters and have fun earning points in the process. Prehistoric adventures can be experienced in the Dino Rise game world, in which the umdasch digital experts have used projectors to create an audiovisual animation. In another themed area, children can use a touchscreen to steer a spaceship through space on an intergalactic space mission, solving various tasks along the way. An event stage and a bistro have also been integrated into the concept.

Where shop windows decorated for Christmas used to make children's eyes light up, this is achieved now by Puppenkönig: an experience-orientated meeting place for children and their parents in the middle of Bonn's city centre.

BUILDINGS

160

140

152

148

134

160

134

148

140

156

134

148

144

156

152

DALIAN HUANAN MIXC ONE MALL

LOCATION DALIAN, CHINA   **CLIENT** CHINA RESOURCES LAND LIMITED, SHENZHEN   **CONCEPT / DESIGN** IPPOLITO FLEITZ GROUP – IDENTITY ARCHITECTS, STUTTGART   **LIGHTING** HAN DU ASSOCIATES, CHONGQING (PLANNING)   **OTHERS** CALLISONRTKL, AMSTERDAM (ARCHITECTURE); PLAND, SHANGHAI (LANDSCAPE ARCHITECTURE); HAMEN, XIAMEN (LOCAL DESIGN INSTITUTE)   **PHOTOGRAPHS** STUDIOSZ PHOTO, SHANGHAI

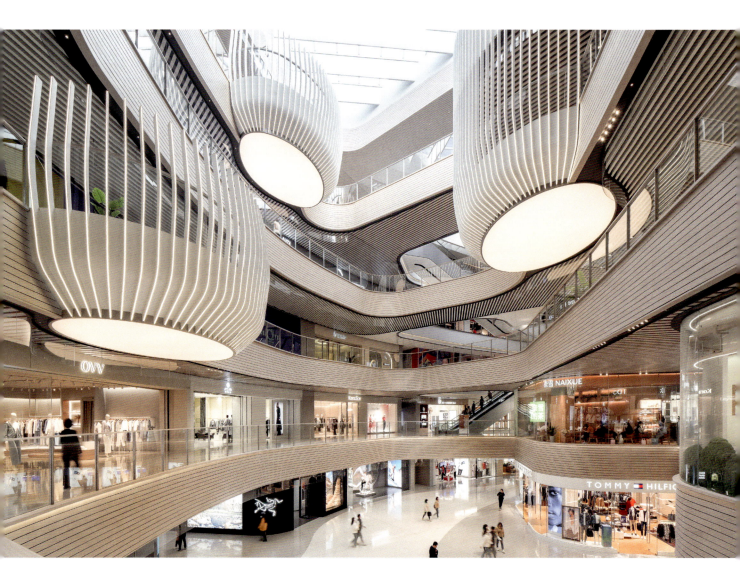

Entspannt wie ein Spaziergang am Meer, so sollen sich vor allem junge Familien fühlen, die sich in der rasant wachsenden Stadt Dalian im Nordosten Chinas, am Golf von Bohai, niederlassen. Dank seiner reizvollen Lage in der Küstenregion gilt der Hafen- und Tourismusort als die „romantische Stadt Nordostchinas". Das für CR Land (China Resources Group) entwickelte Quartier mit der Dalian Huanan MixC One Mall befindet sich außerhalb der Innenstadt und soll zum neuen urbanen Zentrum der Millionenstadt werden.

As relaxed as a seaside stroll – that's how young families should feel when they move to the fast-growing city of Dalian in northeast China, on the Gulf of Bohai. Thanks to its charming coastal location, the port and tourist town is known as the "romantic city of northeast China". The district developed for CR Land (China Resources Group), including the Dalian Huanan MixC One Mall, is located outside the city centre and is set to become the new urban heart of the megacity.

Mit der 84.000 Quadratmeter großen Mall, die Raum für rund 260 Stores bietet, soll ein sozialer Ort geschaffen werden, der konsequent aus dem Blickwinkel der zukünftigen Nutzerschaft heraus entwickelt wurde. Die charakteristische Küstenlandschaft der Gegend, mit der sich vor allem die einheimische Bevölkerung identifiziert, bildet das Leitmotiv der Gestaltung: „Unser Konzept nimmt den Charme der Küstenkulisse mit ihren vorgelagerten Felseninseln auf und positioniert die neue Mall als ‚Insel der Wunder'", so das multidisziplinäre Studio für Gestaltung Ippolito Fleitz Group.

The 84,000-square-metre mall, with space for around 260 stores, is designed to create a social space that is consistently developed from the perspective of future users. The characteristic coastal landscape of the area, with which the local population in particular identifies, forms the leitmotif of the design: "Our concept takes up the charm of the coastal scenery with its offshore rocky islands and positions the new mall as an 'island of wonders'", says the multidisciplinary design studio Ippolito Fleitz Group.

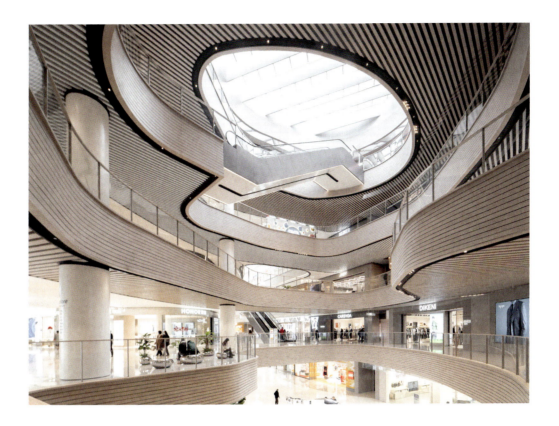

Analog zur reizvollen Küstenlinie Dalians wird der Besucherschaft eine abwechslungsreiche Entdeckungsreise geboten. Alle Hauptareale der Mall haben dabei eine eigene „Sehenswürdigkeit", die es zu erkunden gilt. Die Bezüge zu den regionalen Natur- und Landschaftsthemen reichen von Unterwasserhöhlen über Klippen mit Vogelnestern bis hin zum sternenklaren Himmel. Visuelle Highlights der Mall sind die beeindruckenden Atrien, die dank großzügiger Oberlichter von natürlichem Licht durchflutet sind. Die einzelnen Ebenen sind in organischen Formen vielfältig um den Luftraum modelliert. So schichten sich die Atrien wie die unregelmäßigen Versprünge einer Felsinsel in die Höhe. Gleichzeitig entstehen auf den verschiedenen vertikalen Niveaus Sichtbeziehungen zwischen den Galerien.

In keeping with Dalian's charming coastline, visitors are offered a varied journey of discovery. Each main area of the mall has its own 'attraction' to explore. References to the regional nature and landscape themes range from underwater caves and cliffs with bird nests to the starry sky. The visual highlights of the mall are the impressive atriums, which are flooded with natural light thanks to generous skylights. The individual levels are modelled in a variety of organic shapes around the air space. The atriums are stacked upwards like the irregular projections of a rocky island. At the same time, visual relationships are created between the galleries on the various vertical levels.

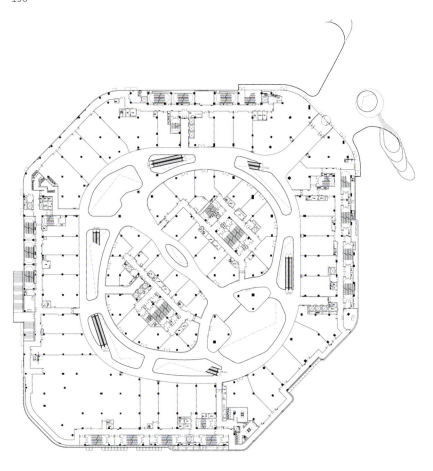

Auch das Materialkonzept weckt maritime Assoziationen. Helle Lattungen an Wänden und Deckenbereichen erinnern an in der Sonne verwittertes Holz, an Stege, die ins Wasser führen, oder an den Rumpf eines Bootes. Die Lamellen in der Deckenverkleidung sind unterschiedlich breit und in verschiedenen Winkeln ausgerichtet. Wie eine Haut legen sich die Holzstrukturen um Atrien und Balkone, sodass trotz der Größe der Räume ein Gefühl von Geborgenheit entstehen kann.

The material concept also evokes maritime associations. Light-coloured battens on the walls and ceilings are reminiscent of wood weathered by the sun, walkways leading into the water or the hull of a boat. The slats used in the ceiling cladding vary in width and angle. The wooden structures wrap around the atriums and balconies like a skin, creating a feeling of cosiness despite the size of the spaces.

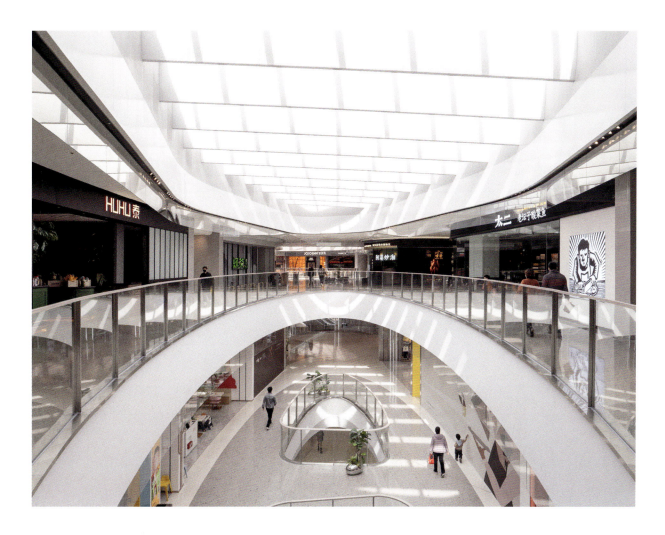

Es gibt also viele Gründe für die jungen chinesischen Familien, sich vor Ort zu verabreden und neue Erlebnisse zu teilen. Die Dalian Huanan MixC One Mall soll zu einem Ort sozialer Begegnung im neuen Stadtviertel werden. „Wo sich Märkte, Zielgruppen, Arbeitswelten oder das Einkaufsverhalten wandeln, ist Auseinandersetzung entscheidend. Pingpong von Sichtweisen und Ansatzpunkten, agiles und direktes Miteinander, Feststellen von Möglichkeiten statt Festhalten an Zuständen. Das nennen wir Status go", so die Gestalter.

So there are plenty of reasons for young Chinese families to get together there and share new experiences. The Dalian Huanan MixC One Mall looks set to become a social meeting place in the new district. "When markets, target groups, working environments or shopping behaviour are changing, discussion is crucial. A ping-pong of perspectives and starting points, agile and direct cooperation, identifying opportunities rather than clinging to the status quo. That's what we call 'status go'," say the designers.

HAGEMEYER

LOCATION MINDEN, GERMANY **CLIENT** HAGEMEYER RETAIL GMBH & CO. KG, MINDEN **CONCEPT / DESIGN** BLOCHER PARTNERS, STUTTGART **LIGHTING** ELAN BELEUCHTUNGS- UND ELEKTROANLAGEN GMBH, COLOGNE **OTHERS** KONRAD KNOBLAUCH GMBH, MARKDORF (SHOPFITTING) **PHOTOGRAPHS** JOACHIM GROTHUS FOTOGRAFIE, HERFORD

Bereits beim Blick durch die großen Schaufenster lässt sich die neue Sportwelt im Mode- und Lifestylehaus Hagemeyer in Minden bestaunen. Als Magnet inmitten der belebten Fußgängerzone gelegen, bietet das traditionsreiche Bekleidungshaus ein Einkaufserlebnis mit fünf Etagen auf rund 19.000 Quadratmetern. Teil des Hagemeyer-Areals ist das denkmalgeschützte Haus Hagemeyer im Stil der Weserrenaissance, von dem der prächtige Vordergiebel erhalten geblieben ist.

The new sports world at the Hagemeyer fashion and lifestyle store in Minden can be admired through the large shop windows even before entering the shop. Situated in the middle of the lively pedestrian zone to draw customers into the city centre, the traditional clothing store offers a shopping experience on around 19,000 square metres spread over five floors. Part of the Hagemeyer site is the listed Hagemeyer House in the Weser Renaissance style, the magnificent front gable of which has been preserved.

 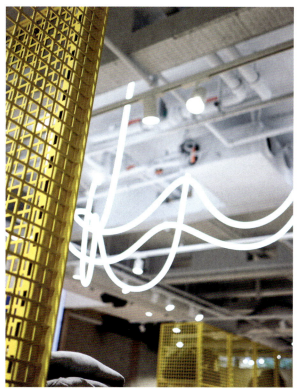

Während des laufenden Betriebs haben blocher partners für das Unternehmen eine dynamische Sportwelt konzipiert, in der die Kundschaft mit großen Schaufenstern und halbtransparenten Wänden empfangen wird – ein weiteres Kapitel der erfolgreichen Zusammenarbeit, die bereits seit 2009 besteht. Stahlgitter und Grafikelemente bilden eine dynamische Präsentationsfläche für die Produkte. In der Damenabteilung prägt eine spezielle rötliche Ton-in-Ton-Installation die warme und ansprechende Umgebung.

Without closing for the refitting, blocher partners created a dynamic sports world for the store, welcoming customers with large shop windows and semi-transparent walls – another chapter in the successful collaboration that began back in 2009. Steel grilles and graphic elements provide a dynamic presentation surface for the products. In the women's department, a specially designed monochrome reddish installation creates a warm and inviting environment.

Das Untergeschoss ist der Outdoor- und Bergsportwelt gewidmet und wurde mit Holz und anderen natürlichen Materialien gestaltet. Durch den Einsatz einer Sonderdecke aus Holzlamellen sowie spezieller Lichtinstallationen haben die Innenarchitekten eine angenehme Raumwirkung geschaffen und die niedrige Deckenhöhe zumindest visuell aufgelöst. Blickachsen und Licht- und Bodeninstallationen führen die Kundschaft zusammen mit einer Fokuswand tief in die Sportfläche hinein. Mit viel Liebe fürs Detail wurde Sportequipment in das Retail Design integriert. So ersetzen zum Beispiel Kletterseile die Verbindungselemente bei Warenträgern.

The basement, which is dedicated to the world of outdoor and mountain sports, uses wood and other natural materials. By installing a ceiling made of wooden slats and special lighting fixtures, the interior designers have created a pleasant spatial effect and overcome the low ceiling height, at least optically. Visual axes, lighting and floor installations, together with a focus wall, guide customers into the heart of the sports area. Sports equipment has been integrated into the retail design with great attention to detail. For example, climbing ropes replace the connecting elements on product carriers.

BUILDINGS   HAGEMEYER

Ein besonderes Highlight ist die Holzwand, auf die eine Bergstruktur gelasert wurde, um die Wanderschuhe effektvoll zu inszenieren. Auf einer Teststrecke mit unterschiedlichen Untergründen können die Schuhe direkt probiert werden. Wandgrafiken in den Umkleidekabinen versetzen das Publikum in Stimmung für das nächste Outdoor-Abenteuer.

A particular highlight is the wooden wall, which has a mountain structure lasered into it to showcase the hiking boots to great effect. The shoes can even be tried out directly on a test track with different surfaces. Wall graphics in the changing rooms set the mood for the next outdoor adventure.

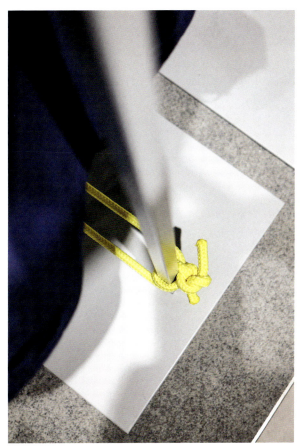

EDEKA ADEBAHR

LOCATION HERZOGENRATH, GERMANY **CLIENT** EDEKA ADEBAHR, HERZOGENRATH
CONCEPT / DESIGN GEORG HEGER / PLANUNGSGRUPPE RHEIN RUHR, ESSEN **LIGHTING** ANSORG GMBH, MÜLHEIM A.D. RUHR
OTHERS PLANUNGSGRUPPE RHEIN RUHR, ESSEN (SHOPFITTING) **PHOTOGRAPHS** BORIS GOLZ, ARNSBERG

Bis 1978 parkten Bahnen und Busse im ehemaligen Straßenbahndepot von Herzogenrath-Kohlscheid, in der Nähe der riesigen Kohleabbaugebiete von Nordrhein-Westfalen. Gleich im Anschluss daran wurde die beeindruckende Halle jahrzehntelang als Supermarkt genutzt. Nun hat die Betreiberfamilie Adebahr ihren Edeka-Markt in dem 120 Jahre alten Gebäude grundlegend revitalisiert, um ein neues, auf die gestiegenen Ansprüche der Kundschaft angepasstes Einkaufserlebnis zu schaffen.

Until 1978, the former tram depot in Herzogenrath-Kohlscheid, close to the vast coal-mining areas of North Rhine-Westphalia, housed streetcars and buses. Immediately afterwards, the impressive hall was used as a supermarket for decades. Now, the Adebahr family has completely revitalised their Edeka store in the 120-year-old building to create a new shopping experience that meets the higher expectations of customers.

BUILDINGS   EDEKA ADEBAHR

„Ziel war es, einen modernen Lebensmittelmarkt mit dem historischen Charme des ehemaligen Steinkohlereviers zu verbinden und dabei gleichzeitig die Gastlichkeit beim Einkauf in den Vordergrund zu stellen", erklärt Lebensmitteleinzelhändler Felix Adebahr.

Die authentischen Architekturelemente standen beim Umbau im Fokus. So wurden große Deckenbereiche mit den originalen Stahlträgerkonstruktionen freigelegt und die seitlichen Fensterbögen geöffnet. Die neu gewonnene Raumhöhe und das Klinkermauerwerk stellten besondere Herausforderungen an die Lichtplanung im Rahmen des Ladenbaus. „Auf den 1.935 Quadratmetern entsprach fast nichts einer üblichen Verkaufsfläche im klassischen Lebensmitteleinzelhandel. Gleichzeitig waren die Ansprüche an das Beleuchtungskonzept hochgesteckt", betont Yvonne Frölich, Head of Lighting Design bei Ansorg aus Mülheim an der Ruhr.

"The aim was to combine a modern grocery store with the historical flair of the former coal-mining area and at the same time focus on hospitality when shopping," explains food retailer Felix Adebahr.

The authentic architectural elements were the focus of the conversion. Large ceiling areas with the original steel girders were exposed and the side window arches were opened. The newly gained room height and the clinker brickwork posed particular challenges for the lighting design of the shopfitting project. "There was almost nothing on the 1,935 square metres that corresponded to a standard shop floor of a traditional food retailer. At the same time, the demands on the lighting concept were high," emphasises Yvonne Frölich, Head of Lighting Design at Ansorg from Mülheim an der Ruhr.

Für die Kundschaft sollte ein offenes Raumgefühl geschaffen, das Sortiment von etwa 25.000 Artikeln ohne Verschattungen ausgeleuchtet und die Waren bei einer warmen Lichtatmosphäre akzentuiert werden. Um dies zu ermöglichen, wurden die Leuchten auf einer Höhe von 4,20 Metern, etwa einen Meter oberhalb der üblichen Aufhängung, positioniert. Damit die Flächenbeleuchtung ohne Schattenbildung funktioniert, verzichteten die Lichtexperten auf lineare Beleuchtungssysteme und es wurden Reflektorleuchten eingesetzt.

The aim was to create a sense of spaciousness for customers, to illuminate the range of around 25,000 items without shadows and to accentuate the goods in a warm lighting atmosphere. To achieve this, the lights were positioned at a height of 4.20 metres, that is about one metre above the usual suspension point. To ensure that the area lighting works without casting any shadows, the lighting experts dispensed with linear lighting systems and instead used reflector luminaires.

Zurück zu den Wurzeln: In Anlehnung an das Verkehrsnetz im ÖPNV hat man die verschiedenen Abteilungen in Anlehnung an Haltestationen der Straßenbahnen und Busse benannt. Unterstrichen wird das Gesamtkonzept durch großformatige Fotos aus der Kaiserzeit, der Industrialisierung und den frühen Tagen des Steinkohleabbaus.

Back to the roots: With reference to the public transport network, the various departments are named after tram and bus stops. The overall concept is underpinned by large-format photos of late 19th century imperial Germany, industrialisation and the early days of coal mining.

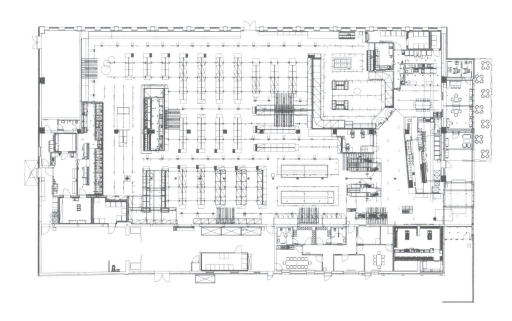

KRÖPELINER STRASSE 64

LOCATION ROSTOCK, GERMANY   **CLIENT** J. HOEPP, OLDENBURG   **CONCEPT / DESIGN** ATP ARCHITEKTEN INGENIEURE, NUREMBERG   **PHOTOGRAPHS** ATP ARCHITEKTEN INGENIEURE, NUREMBERG / HOLGER MARTENS, ROSTOCK

Als „Rostocks schönstes Kaufhaus" ist die historische Villa in der Kröpeliner Straße 64 weit über die Stadtgrenzen hinaus bekannt. Nach vielen Jahren des Leerstands sollte diese wieder in ihrem alten Glanz erstrahlen und ein attraktives Einkaufserlebnis bieten. Mit viel Fingerspitzengefühl und einem sensiblen denkmalpflegerischen Konzept hauchte ATP architekten ingenieure dem Kaufhaus wieder neues Leben ein.

The historic villa at Kröpeliner Strasse 64 was known far beyond the city limits as 'Rostock's most beautiful department store'. After standing empty for many years, it was to be restored to its former glory and offer an attractive shopping experience. ATP architekten ingenieure breathed new life into the store with great finesse and a sensitive conservation concept.

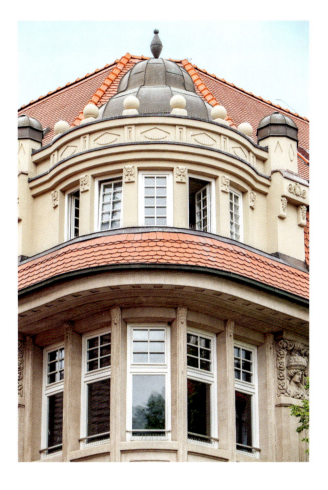

Das Gebäude entstand 1910/11 nach dem Entwurf des Architekten Paul Korff und ist ein wichtiges Zeitzeugnis früher Stahlbetonbauten. Ursprünglich für den Rostocker Kaufmann Franz Schurig als Modekaufhaus errichtet, erwarb die Rostocker Kaufmannsfamilie von Gustaf Zeeck die Immobilie und eröffnete dort 1930 einen Teppichladen. Durch eine Fliegerbombe im Jahr 1942 wurde das Haus stark beschädigt. Dabei gingen neben den Dachaufbauten auch die markanten Bauformen verloren. Lediglich die Attika mit der bekrönenden Eckbetonung blieb erhalten. Seither wurden diverse unsensible Sanierungseingriffe ohne Rücksicht auf die Geschichtsträchtigkeit des Gebäudes vorgenommen. Nach sechs Jahren Leerstand sollte nun der unter Denkmalschutz stehende Bau wieder zum „Schmuckkästchen" der Rostocker Innenstadt werden.

The building was constructed in 1910/11 to a design by architect Paul Korff and is an important example of early reinforced concrete construction. Originally built as a fashion department store for the Rostock merchant Franz Schurig, the building was acquired by the Rostock merchant family of Gustaf Zeeck who opened a carpet store there in 1930. The building was heavily bombed in 1942. In addition to the roof structures, the distinctive architectural forms were also lost. Only the parapet with the crowning corner accent remained. Since then, various heavy-handed renovations have been carried out without regard for the historical significance of the house. After six years of vacancy, the listed building was to become the jewel of Rostock's city centre once again.

ATP architekten ingenieure entwickelte für den Auftraggeber J. Hoepp ein ganzheitliches Architekturkonzept. Im denkmalpflegerischen Leitbild legte das Planungsteam besonderen Wert auf den Erhalt der historischen Bausubstanz und eine behutsame Sanierung. Die Primärtragstruktur sowie die sogenannte „Korff-Fassade" sollten erhalten bleiben. Daher wurde die Fassade nur in Teilbereichen ausgebessert und es wurden überflüssige Lasten behutsam aus dem Gebäude entfernt. Bei den vorsichtigen Um- und Weiterbaumaßnahmen kam auch der beeindruckende Skelettbau wieder zum Vorschein.

ATP architekten ingenieure developed a holistic architectural concept for the client J. Hoepp. In the conservation guidelines, the design team placed particular emphasis on preserving the historic building fabric and careful refurbishment. The primary load-bearing structure and the "Korff façade" were to be retained. The façade was therefore only partially repaired and superfluous loads were carefully removed from the building. The impressive skeleton structure also reappeared during the careful conversion and further construction work.

The revitalisation and re-letting of the historic department store has brought a noticeable boost to Rostock's city centre. A long queue formed right across the pedestrian zone on the opening day of the Rituals store. Visitors now enter a contemporary interior through the striking, copper-roofed entrance, which has nevertheless retained its historical charm.

Durch die Revitalisierung und Neuvermietung des historischen Kaufhauses wird die Rostocker Innenstadt nun spürbar belebt. Schon am Eröffnungstag des Rituals-Stores bildete sich eine lange Schlange quer durch die Fußgängerzone. Über den markanten, kupferdachgekrönten Eingang gelangen Besuchende jetzt in einen zeitgemäßen Innenraum, der dennoch seinen historischen Charme bewahrt hat.

PALLADIUM MALL AHMEDABAD

LOCATION AHMEDABAD, INDIA **CLIENT** PHOENIX MILL & B SAFAL GROUP, AHMEDABAD **CONCEPT / DESIGN** BLOCHER PARTNERS, STUTTGART / AHMEDABAD **PHOTOGRAPHS** ATIK BHEDA PHOTOGRAPHY, AHMEDABAD

Indien ist mit seinen über 1,4 Milliarden Einwohnern eines der bevölkerungsreichsten Länder der Erde. Mit einer boomenden Start-up-Szene, rasantem Wirtschaftswachstum und gut ausgebildeten Fachkräften ist das Land auf dem besten Weg, zu einem der größten Konsumgütermärkte weltweit zu werden.

With over 1.4 billion inhabitants, India is one of the most populous countries in the world. A booming start-up scene, rapid economic growth and a well-trained workforce mean that the country is well on its way to becoming one of the largest consumer goods markets in the world.

Im Herzen der indischen Millionenmetropole Ahmedabad haben die Architekten von blocher partners india die erste Luxus-Shoppingmall des Bundesstaats Gujarat entworfen. Die Stadt Ahmedabad hat sich nicht nur zum größten Handelszentrum im Westen Indiens entwickelt, sondern ist seit 2017 auch als UNESCO Weltkulturerbe anerkannt.

Die Palladium Mall ist das größte Einkaufszentrum vor Ort und steht für Luxus, Stil und Eleganz. Die Architektur und das Retail Design schaffen eine eindrucksvolle Einkaufskulisse für Einheimische und Touristen. Durch die Aufteilung des Bauvolumens in drei Teile entsteht eine markante Kubatur, die sich dem menschlichen Maßstab anpassen soll. Die überwiegend geschlossene Fassade ist mit kleinteiligen Metallschindeln, die reflektierende und nichtreflektierende Oberflächen haben, verkleidet. Je nach Sonneneinstrahlung, Blickwinkel und Tageszeit verändert die gesamte Mall dadurch ihr Erscheinungsbild.

In the heart of the Indian metropolis of Ahmedabad, the architects from blocher partners india have designed the first luxury shopping mall in the state of Gujarat. The city of Ahmedabad has not only developed into the largest commercial centre in western India. Since 2017 it has also been a UNESCO World Heritage Site.

The Palladium Mall is the largest shopping centre in the city and stands for luxury, style and elegance. The architecture and retail design make for an impressive shopping experience for locals and tourists alike. The division of the building volume into three parts creates a striking cubature that is intended to adapt to the human scale. The predominantly closed façade is clad with small metal shingles with reflective and non-reflective surfaces. Depending on the sunlight, viewing angle and time of day, the entire mall changes its appearance.

Das Innere ist durch großzügige Atrien strukturiert, die nicht nur als Orientierungspunkte dienen, sondern durch Begrünung, Wasserelemente und Kunstwerke auch zum Verweilen einladen. Dies wird auf den fünf Etagen nicht nur durch die Auswahl internationaler und nationaler Marken, sondern auch durch vielfältige Cafés, Restaurants und Unterhaltungsangebote unterstrichen. Viele Elemente aus Naturstein, Bronze und Gold sowie Details wie intarsierte Marmorböden betonen den luxuriösen Charakter.

The interior is structured by spacious atriums that not only serve as orientation points, but also invite visitors to linger to enjoy the greenery, water features and artwork. This is underlined not only by the selection of international and national labels and brands on the five floors, but also by the wide range of cafés, restaurants and entertainment venues. Many elements made of natural stone, bronze and gold as well as details such as inlaid marble floors add to the luxurious feel.

Die Palladium Mall ist das erste Projekt, das blocher partners india in Zusammenarbeit mit Phoenix Mills Ltd aus Mumbai und der ortsansässigen B Safal Group realisiert haben. Ein weiteres Shopppingcenter in der Diamantenstadt Surat (Gujarat) ist derzeit in Planung.

The Palladium Mall is the first project realised by blocher partners india in cooperation with Phoenix Mills Ltd of Mumbai and the local B Safal Group. Another shopping centre is currently being planned in the diamond city of Surat (Gujarat).

RÄBGASS SHOPPING CENTER

LOCATION BASLE, SWITZERLAND   **CLIENT** SWISS PRIME SITE IMMOBILIEN AG, ZUG   **CONCEPT / DESIGN** MINT ARCHITECTURE, ZURICH, PART OF THE ATP GROUP   **PHOTOGRAPHS** OLIVER RUST | KO GMBH, ZURICH

Second Life für ein 40 Jahre altes Einkaufszentrum – mit erfolgreicher Revitalisierung, neuem hochwertigem Wohnraum und einer nachhaltigen Gebäudesanierung transformierten Mint Architecture das in die Jahre gekommene Shoppingcenter in eine zeitgemäße Mixed-Use-Immobilie.

Second life for a 40-year-old shopping centre – with a successful revitalisation, new high-quality living space and a sustainable building refurbishment, Mint Architecture transformed the ageing shopping centre into a contemporary mixed-use property.

BUILDINGS RÄBGASS SHOPPING CENTER

Das Räbgass Center in Basel steht exemplarisch für die Entwicklung vieler in den 1980er-Jahren erbauter Einkaufszentren. Es beherbergte bis Mitte der 90er-Jahre ein renommiertes Warenhaus. Nach dessen Auszug verlor es an Attraktivität und Glanz und es genügte auch den baulichen Anforderungen nicht mehr.

Als sich eine große Detailhandelskette für das Räbgass entschied, wurde Mint Architecture damit beauftragt, das Einkaufszentrum zu sanieren, um den Leerstand zu beheben. Mit Blick auf eine ökonomische und ökologische Aufwertung entwickelte das Strategie- und Planungsbüro eine Mischnutzung, einhergehend mit einer Totalsanierung des Gebäudes. Die Retailflächen wurden neu ausgelegt und die Mall modernisiert. Dank der neuen Aufteilung entstanden auf drei Etagen großzügige Verkaufsflächen. Diese umsäumen die sanierte Mall, die durch die Versetzung des Eingangs und der Rolltreppe ein großzügiges und helles Ambiente erhält.

The Räbgass Center in Basle is an example of the development of many shopping centres built in the 1980s. Until the mid-1990s, it housed a well-known department store. After it moved out, however, it lost its attractiveness and splendour and no longer met the structural requirements.

When a major grocery chain chose Räbgass, Mint Architecture was commissioned to renovate the shopping centre to eliminate the vacancy. With a view to economic and ecological upgrading, the strategy and design office developed a mixed-use concept, accompanied by a total refurbishment of the building. The retail areas were redesigned and the mall was modernised. The new layout has created generous retail space on three floors. These surround the refurbished mall, which has been given a spacious and bright ambience thanks to the relocation of the entrance and escalator.

Im hinteren Teil sorgt ein freundliches, mit warmem Holz gestaltetes Selbstbedienungscafé für neue Aufenthaltsqualität. Den ungenutzten 850 Quadratmeter großen Hohlraum im Dachgeschoss verwandelte man in eine Wohnetage mit sechs Loftwohnungen. Diese sind offen gestaltet, bieten jeweils ein Patio und eine Terrasse und sind durch einen separaten Lift zugänglich. Silbern gestrichene, die Technik freilegende Betondecken verleihen den Wohnungen Großstadtflair, das mit warmen Böden aus Eichenparkett kontrastiert. Die Fassade aus Waschbeton der 80er-Jahre wurde gereinigt und in einem hellen Beige neu gestrichen. Die zusätzlichen Fensterfronten, die einheitliche Signaletik und das neue Brand Design verleihen dem Räbgass Center ein wertiges Außenbild, wodurch sich das Einkaufszentrum wieder in die gepflegte Häuserzeile der Basler Innenstadt einfügt.

At the rear, a friendly self-service café designed in warm woods provides a new quality of stay. The unused 850 square-metre space in the roof has been transformed into a residential floor with six loft apartments. They are open-plan, each with a patio and terrace and are accessed via a separate lift. Silver-painted concrete ceilings that expose the technology lend the apartments a metropolitan flair that contrasts with warm oak parquet floors. The exposed concrete façade from the 1980s was cleaned and repainted in a light beige. The additional window frontage, uniform signage and a new brand design give the Räbgass Center a high-quality appearance and allow it to blend in again with the well-kept row of buildings in Basle's city centre.

The property, which includes a shopping centre, parking facilities and residential floor, meets the latest Swiss quality standards for energy-conscious construction (Minergie), including thermal insulation, air tightness, photovoltaics, ventilation systems and lighting. The solar park installed on the roof supplies electricity for a large part of the shopping centre's building services requirements. The partial greening of the roof and the branches ensure the required biodiversity.

Die Liegenschaft mit Einkaufszentrum, Parkmöglichkeiten und Wohnetage entspricht den jüngsten Minergiestandards, was die Wärmedämmung, die Luftdichtheit, Photovoltaik, Belüftungssysteme und die Beleuchtung umfasst. Der auf dem Dach realisierte Solarpark liefert Strom für einen Großteil des Haustechnikbedarfs des Einkaufszentrums. Durch die Teilbegrünung des Daches und das Astwerk wird der geforderten Biodiversität Rechnung getragen.

WOLLHAUS HEILBRONN

LOCATION HEILBRONN, GERMANY   **CLIENT** NEUFELD IMMOBILIEN, OEDHEIM
CONCEPT / DESIGN BLOCHER PARTNERS, STUTTGART   **VISUALISATIONS** BLOCHER PARTNERS, STUTTGART

Das Heilbronner Wollhaus ist mit seinem zehnstöckigen Büroturm und dem flacheren, asymmetrischen Kaufhaustrakt ein typisches Beispiel für die verkehrsgerechte Verdichtung der Innenstädte in den 1970er-Jahren.

Nur der Name des innerstädtischen Einkaufszentrums nimmt noch Bezug auf den dort früher stattgefundenen württembergischen Wollmarkt. Die gesellschaftlichen wie auch wirtschaftlichen Veränderungen der letzten Jahre führten dazu, dass das massiv bebaute Areal am Busbahnhof zum Sorgenkind der Heilbronner Innenstadt geworden ist.

With its ten-storey office tower and the flatter, asymmetrical department store wing, the Heilbronn Wollhaus is a typical example of the traffic-orientated densification of city centres in the 1970s.

Only the name of the inner-city shopping centre still refers to the Württemberg wool market that used to take place there. Both the social and the economic changes of recent years have turned the once densely built-up zone around the bus station into the problem area of Heilbronn's city centre.

Das Stuttgarter Planungsbüro blocher partners ist angetreten, das in die Jahre gekommene Wollhaus in einen lebendigen Stadtbaustein zu transformieren. Entgegen der von vielen Seiten zu hörenden Rufe nach einem Abriss nutzt das Konzept der Architekten bewusst die verdeckten Potenziale der bestehenden Bausubstanz. Es gilt, die Qualitäten des vorhandenen Stadtbausteins zu erkennen und sinnvoll zu ergänzen.

Anstelle von Abriss und Neubau soll das alte Wollhaus in ein energiepositives Quartier transformiert werden. Die Idee folgt dem Cradle-to-Cradle-Ansatz, nach dem die Stadt mit ihren Bauten als Materiallager verstanden wird. Großen Wert legen die Planer auf die Rückbaufähigkeit des Gebäudes und die nachhaltige Auswahl der Materialien.

The Stuttgart-based architects blocher partners have set out to transform the run-down Wollhaus into a lively component of the city. Contrary to many calls for demolition, the architects' concept instead leverages the hidden potential of the existing building fabric. The aim is to recognise its existing qualities and complement them in a meaningful way.

Instead of demolition and new build, the old Wollhaus is to be transformed into an energy-positive district. The idea follows the cradle-to-cradle approach which sees the city and its buildings as a warehouse of materials. For the designers, it is very important that the building is designed to be dismantled or rebuilt. The materials chosen should also be sustainable.

Das Konzept sieht nur minimale Rückbaumaßnahmen vor und legt den Fokus stattdessen auf Um- und Weiterbau. So werden sich ein Wohnriegel und ein Hotel auf den Bestand setzen. Graue Energie wird gebunden und die Aufstockung erfolgt durch ein Holzhybridtragwerk. Eine Photovoltaikanlage auf dem Dach dient als hauseigenes Kraftwerk. Begrünte Dächer fördern in Kombination mit intelligentem Regenwassermanagement eine hohe Biodiversität und bieten Flächen zur Erholung. Außerdem macht sich das Konzept die Vorteile des modularen Bauens zunutze, wodurch Bauzeit und Lärmbelästigung effektiv reduziert werden können.

Das Team von blocher partners entwickelt die Vision einer sich gegenseitig befruchtenden Mischnutzung: Neben einem Nahversorger wird es Ladenflächen geben sowie Wohnungen, Hotellerie, Büros, Gesundheits- und Fitnessangebote, auch eine Kindertagesstätte ist angedacht. Durch diese Vielfalt soll das Gebäude wieder zu einem integralen Bestandteil der Stadt werden.

The concept envisages only minimal demolition measures, focusing instead on conversions and additions. A residential block and a hotel will be built on top of the existing building. This will conserve grey energy and the extension will be a hybrid timber structure. A photovoltaic system on the roof serves as the building's own power station. Combined with intelligent rainwater management, the green roof promotes a high level of biodiversity and provides areas for recreation. The concept also makes use of the advantages of modular construction, which can effectively reduce construction time and noise pollution.

The blocher partners team is developing a vision of mutually beneficial mixed use: In addition to a local supermarket, there will be retail space as well as apartments, hotels, offices, health and fitness facilities, and a day care centre is also planned. This diversity is intended to make the building an integral part of the city once again.

BUILDINGS   WOLLHAUS HEILBRONN

Gebaut werden könnte ab 2026, die Eröffnung ist für 2028 geplant. Der Bauherr, die Neufeld Immobilien GmbH, plant die Zeit bis zum Baubeginn bestmöglich zu überbrücken und das Umfeld zu stärken, heißt es in den Nachrichten der Stadt Heilbronn. So könnten im Erdgeschoss in der Zeit der Zwischennutzung wieder Händler einziehen. Außerdem wird geprüft, ob Freizeitangebote für Familien, aber auch für Erwachsene und Jugendliche im Obergeschoss zu realisieren sind und das Untergeschoss zeitweise für Ausstellungen genutzt werden kann.

Construction could begin in 2026, with the opening planned for 2028. According to news reports from the city of Heilbronn, the client, Neufeld Immobilien GmbH, wants to bridge the time until the start of construction in the best possible way and to strengthen the surrounding area. This would allow retailers to move back into the ground floor during the period of interim use. Other options being considered include leisure activities for families, adults and young people on the upper floor and temporary exhibitions in the basement.

THE AUTHORS

RETAIL DESIGN INTERNATIONAL VOL. 9

Dr. Jons Messedat

studierte Architektur an der RWTH Aachen, der Universität Stuttgart und als Stipendiat an der London South Bank University. Parallel dazu machte er sein Diplom als Industriedesigner bei Richard Sapper. Es folgte eine Hochschulassistenz an der Bauhaus-Universität Weimar, die er 2004 mit der Promotion zum Thema Corporate Architecture abschloss. Im Büro von Sir Norman Foster plante er das heutige Red Dot Design Museum in Essen und das Interior Design im Reichstagsgebäude in Berlin. Als zertifizierter Preisrichter wirkt er in internationalen Architektur- und Designwettbewerben mit. Seit 2016 lehrt er das Fach Bau und Raum an der HAWK Hochschule für angewandte Wissenschaft und Kunst Hildesheim. Er war Jurymitglied im Wettbewerb für das bauliche Corporate Design im Berliner Humboldt Forum und wurde 2018 von der Architektenkammer Niedersachsen in die Jury zum Staatspreis für Architektur berufen. Im Beirat der Mia Seeger Stiftung engagiert er sich seit 2023 in der Förderung junger Designtalente.
www.messedat.com

Dr. Jons Messedat

studied architecture at the RWTH Aachen University, the University of Stuttgart and had a scholarship to the London South Bank University. In parallel, he qualified as industrial designer under Richard Sapper. This was followed by a university assistantship at the Bauhaus University Weimar, which he completed in 2004 with a doctorate in the field of Corporate Architecture. In the office of Sir Norman Foster he worked on the design of today's Red Dot Design Museum in Essen and was responsible for the interior design of the Reichstag building in Berlin. As certified competition judge, he is involved in a number of international architecture and design competitions. Since 2016, he has been teaching the building and space module at the HAWK University of applied sciences and art in Hildesheim. He was on the panel for built Corporate Design in the Berlin Humboldt Forum and in 2018 was appointed onto the jury of the state prize for architecture by the chamber of architects for the federal state of Lower Saxony. On the advisory board of the Mia Seeger Foundation, he has been involved in promoting young design talent since 2023.
www.messedat.com

Albert Achammer

Nach beruflichen Lehr- und Wanderjahren bei unterschiedlichen Stationen in der Immobilienindustrie und bei gmp – Von Gerkan, Marg und Partner in Hamburg gründete Albert Achammer einen neuen Standort für ATP architekten ingenieure, Europas führendes Büro für Integrale Planung, in Hamburg. Vier Jahre nach Gründung stellt sich ATP Hamburg mit 60+ Mitarbeitenden aus Architektur- und Ingenieurwesen als erfolgreicher integraler Planer vor. Albert Achammer hält einen Master of Science in Architektur von der ETH Zürich und einen MBA von der IESE Business School.
www.atp.ag

Albert Achammer

After years of professional training and gathering experience in various positions in the real estate industry and at gmp – Von Gerkan, Marg and Partners in Hamburg, Albert Achammer founded a new location for ATP architekten ingenieure, Europe's leading office for integral planning, in Hamburg. Four years after its foundation, ATP Hamburg presents itself as a successful integral planner with more than 60 employees from the fields of architecture and engineering. Albert Achammer holds a Master of Science in Architecture from ETH Zurich and an MBA from IESE Business School.
www.atp.ag

Jutta Blocher

studierte Innenarchitektur an der Hochschule für Technik Stuttgart, arbeitete nach ihrem Studium sechs Jahre beim Planungsbüro R. Czermak und gründete 1989 zusammen mit ihrem Mann Dieter Blocher blocher partners. Von Beginn an bestimmte die Symbiose von Architektur und Innenarchitektur ihre Herangehensweise in der Unternehmensgruppe, was unter anderem 2006 zu den Gründungen von blocher partners shops (spezialisiert auf Monomarken und Retail Consulting) sowie der Kommunikationsagentur typenraum und der asiatischen Dependance blocher partners india (2009) führte. Als Head of Interior Design verantwortet Jutta Blocher vielfältigste nationale wie internationale Projekte und erwarb sich durch eine Gestaltung, die Freiräume für Marken und Identitäten schafft, den Ruf einer Expertin für Markenkommunikation. So begleitete sie viele Department-, Fashion- und Luxus-Stores, aber auch Monomarken. Es folgten etliche Projekte, die über die Architektur hinaus für eine Brand Evolution stehen, also über die formale Gestaltung hinaus Markenidentität kommunizieren. So beispielsweise der Gestaltungsauftrag für Hugo Boss, der Store-Konzepte, Flagship-Stores, Verwaltungsgebäude und Outlets beinhaltet. Unter der Regie von Jutta Blocher weitete das Büro seinen Aktionsradius nach Asien aus: blocher partners realisierte unter anderem Department Stores für namhafte Handelsmarken in Indien, Thailand, Malaysien, Indonesien und auf den Philippinen. Jutta Blocher ist Mitglied im BDIA.
www.blocherpartners.com

Jutta Blocher

studied interior architecture at the Hochschule für Technik Stuttgart, after which she worked for six years at Planungsbüro R. Czermak and in 1989 co-founded blocher partners together with her husband Dieter Blocher. From the outset, the symbiosis of architecture and interior architecture guided the approach of the group, leading amongst others to the formation of blocher partners shops in 2008 (specialised in mono-brands and retail consulting) as well as the communication agency typenraum and the Asian dependency blocher partners india (2009). As Head of Interior Design Jutta Blocher is responsible for a wide range of national and international projects and through a design which creates space for brands and identities acquired a reputation as expert for brand communication. Her customers include department, fashion and luxury stores, but also mono-brands. There followed countless projects that go beyond architecture and stand for a brand evolution, finding ways beyond formal design of communicating brand identity. The design assignment for Hugo Boss is a case in point, including store concepts, flagship stores, administration building and outlets. Jutta Blocher was also the driving force behind the office's expansion into Asia: projects realised there by blocher partners include department stores for well-known retail brands in India, Thailand, Malaysia, and on the Philippines. Jutta Blocher belongs to the German association of interior architects BDIA.
www.blocherpartners.com

THE AUTHORS

Gabi Stumvoll

ist seit 2022 für die Kommunikation der Rid Stiftung und die neuen Förderformate Retail Tour und Retail Talk verantwortlich. Die Diplom-Politologin war über zehn Jahre in verschiedenen Funktionen in internationalen Unternehmen der Immobilienbranche tätig und hat nach ihrem Master in Ökonomie und Management in der Stiftungsverwaltung der Ludwig-Maximilians-Universität und der Immobilienverwaltung der Rid Stiftung gearbeitet. Zuletzt oblag ihr in einem Start-up-Unternehmen der Outdoor-Food-Branche die Verantwortung für die Social-Media-Kommunikation.

Gabi Stumvoll

has been responsible for the communication of the Rid Foundation and the new Retail Tour and Retail Talk funding formats since 2022. The graduate political scientist worked for over ten years in various positions in international companies in the real estate sector. After completing her Master's degree in economics and management, she worked in the foundation administration of the Ludwig Maximilian University and the real estate administration of the Rid Foundation. Most recently, she was responsible for social media communication at a start-up company in the outdoor food industry.

www.rid-stiftung.de
www.futureretailstore.de

Dr. Maximilian Perez

ist seit 2023 für die Rid Stiftung tätig und dort zuständig für den Aufbau des Bereichs Innovationsförderung. Eines der ersten Projekte in diesem Förderbereich ist der Future Retail Store, konzipiert als Experimentierraum für den Handel. Vor seiner Tätigkeit bei der Rid Stiftung war Dr. Perez beim Fraunhofer Institut für Integrierte Schaltungen IIS verantwortlich für das Forschungsfeld Retail Innovation. Zusätzlich zu seiner Tätigkeit in der Rid Stiftung ist er als Dozent an der Technischen Hochschule Augsburg und als Gastdozent an der Friedrich-Alexander-Universität Erlangen-Nürnberg aktiv.

Dr. Maximilian Perez

has been working for the Rid Foundation since 2023, where he is responsible for developing the Innovation Promotion division. One of the first projects in this division is the Future Retail Store, designed as an experimental space for retail. Before joining the Rid Foundation, Dr. Perez was responsible for Retail Innovation at the Fraunhofer Institute for Integrated Circuits IIS. In addition to his work at the Rid Foundation, he is also a lecturer at the Augsburg University of Applied Sciences and a guest lecturer at the Friedrich-Alexander University of Erlangen-Nuremberg.

www.rid-stiftung.de
www.futureretailstore.de

IMPRINT

EDITOR / AUTHOR
Jons Messedat

EDITING / TYPESETTING
Mario Ableitner

TRANSLATION
Beverley Locke, Mario Ableitner

LAYOUT
Tina Agard Grafik & Buchdesign, Stuttgart

LITHOGRAPHY
Paladin Design- und Werbemanufaktur, Remseck

PRINTING
Schleunungdruck, Marktheidenfeld

FONTS
Niveau Grotesk

PAPER
Gardamatt Eleven, 170 g/m^2

COVER PHOTO
Satoshi Shigeta
Maison m-i-d 1985, Osaka
CURIOSITY, Tokyo

PHOTO CREDITS
ATP architekten ingenieure (p. 9–12), blocher partners, Stuttgart (p. 14–19, 132/133, 166), Rid Stiftung /Jürgen Stresius, Munich (p. 20), Rid Stiftung /Jan Schmiedel, Munich (p. 21–23, 167), Jens Pfisterer, Stuttgart (p. 24/25), Jons Messedat, Stuttgart / Lindau (Bodensee) (p. 164), ATP architekten ingenieure / Wang (p. 165)

avedition GmbH
Publishers for Architecture and Design
Senefelderstraße 109
70176 Stuttgart
Germany

Tel.: +49 (0)711 / 220 22 79-0
Fax: +49 (0)711 / 220 22 79-15

retaildesign@avedition.de
www.avedition.com

© Copyright 2024 **av**edition GmbH, Stuttgart

© Copyright of photos with individual companies, agencies and photographers

This work is subject to copyright. All rights are reserved, whether the whole or part of the material is concerned, and specifically but not exclusively the right of translation, reprinting, reuse of illustrations, recitation, broadcasting, reproduction on microfilms or in other ways, and storage in databases or any other media. For use of any kind, the written permission of the copyright owner must be obtained.

ISBN 978-3-89986-426-7